Movements and Positions
in the Battle
of Kennesaw Mountain

Movements and Positions in the Battle of Kennesaw Mountain

The Memoir of Colonel James T. Holmes, 52d Ohio Volunteer Infantry

JAMES T. HOLMES

EDITED BY GARTH D. BISHOP
With an Introduction and Annotations by Mark A. Smith

McFarland & Company, Inc., Publishers
Jefferson, North Carolina

Frontispiece: Col. James Taylor Holmes, ca. 1915 (family archives).

ISBN (print) 978-1-4766-7312-7 ∞
ISBN (ebook) 978-1-4766-3421-0

LIBRARY OF CONGRESS CATALOGUING DATA ARE AVAILABLE

BRITISH LIBRARY CATALOGUING DATA ARE AVAILABLE

© 2018 Garth D. Bishop. All rights reserved

No part of this book may be reproduced or transmitted in any form or by any means, electronic or mechanical, including photocopying or recording, or by any information storage and retrieval system, without permission in writing from the publisher.

Front cover image: *inset* James Taylor Holmes, 52nd Ohio Volunteers (J. B. Work, ed., *Re-Union of Col. Dan McCook's Third Brigade...*, *August, 1900* (Chicago 1901); "Battle of Kenesaw [sic] Mountian [sic] June 27," 1864, Kurz & Allison, circa 1891 (Library of Congress)

Printed in the United States of America

McFarland & Company, Inc., Publishers
Box 611, Jefferson, North Carolina 28640
www.mcfarlandpub.com

To my great-grandfather, Col. James Taylor Holmes;
to each of his descendants, that they should
know the content of his character;
and to all Civil War Historians,
this book is respectfully dedicated.
—Garth D. Bishop

Prologue

The author was a participant in Kenesaw. Developments near the close of a long life have rendered it necessary for him to write these two chapters on certain phases of that battle and prior and subsequent events. The first one was written in November 1903, and the second one in June 1915. There was no thought of the second when the first was written, nor for more than ten years afterward. Each has for its subject only the truth of history and that falsehood, expressed or suggested, shall work no injustice, now or hereafter.—James T. Holmes

Table of Contents

Prologue	viii
Editor's Acknowledgments	x
Preface by Garth D. Bishop	1
Introduction by Mark A. Smith	9
CHAPTER ONE	59
CHAPTER TWO	88
Appendix I	133
Appendix II	138
Annotations	141
Index	153

Editor's Acknowledgments

My sincere thanks and appreciation are extended to:

Professor Mark A. Smith of Fort Valley State University for his thorough knowledge of the battle at Kennesaw, and his keen interest in corroborating Col. Holmes' argument. His contribution to this book was invaluable and essential to its success.

Editor Dylan Lightfoot for his thoughtful ideas, suggestions and genuine interest in this unique project. He and the rest of the staff at McFarland helped make this dream book a reality.

Patti Holmes Ballard and her husband Charles for allowing me into their beautiful home to review letters and documents, to take photographs, and to enjoy the love and respect Patti has for our great-grandfather, Lieutenant Col. James Taylor Holmes. I am grateful that he followed through on the need to put his observations, thoughts and actions in the battle at Kennesaw Mountain into words, for the sake of history—GDB

Preface

BY GARTH D. BISHOP

Constance Mabury Holmes. That was my mother's maiden name. And she was proud of it.

Preferring to be addressed as "Constance" and not "Connie," should you make the mistake and address her as such, you were promptly corrected. Constance was the name which she was given, and that was the one which she would use. Period.

But Holmes was the name of which she was most proud, for her ancestral line included family members who were uniquely devout, courageous and in some cases, famous. It was something of which she was well aware, for it was documented by her grandfather, Col. James Taylor Holmes in a book entitled *The American Family of Rev. Obediah Holmes* (1915). My mother had many original leather bound copies of that book, one of which was signed by its author and is currently in this writer's possession.

Constance Mabury Holmes married Douglas Graham Bishop on March 22, 1941, and they bore three daughters: Elaine Mabury, Diana Graham and Joyce Claire. I am happy to note that in 1954, she convinced my father to try one more time; as she told the story to me over the years, she felt that she "was not yet through." She wanted a son, and she knew that Douglas did too, although he never openly admitted it.

The fourth time proved to be the charm. And when my identical twin brother Quentin Holmes and I were born on October 24, 1954, she would say then, and many times again over the years (with apologies to the great game of poker), "Three of a kind and a pair make a full house."

Preface by Garth D. Bishop

Early on in my upbringing, my mother would refer me to the Holmes family history and to Col. James Taylor (J.T.) Holmes in particular. She would tell me that one of her earliest childhood memories was her sitting on her grandfather's lap, but that no other memories of him had survived. That is entirely understandable, as she was born on February 9, 1914, and the Colonel passed away on February 17, 1916. She would periodically show me pictures of him and bring out his Civil War diary for me to read some of its excerpts, then whisk it away to put back in a special drawer for safe keeping. "It will be yours, someday," she would say. So when my mother passed away from acute leukemia at age 94 on July 24, 2008, the diary would indeed come to me—but not easily.

The small apartment in which she lived was stockpiled to the brim with books, pictures, paintings, silver and antique furniture. Most of it had been accumulated over the years from large homes in which she raised her five children, and had now been condensed into a space a mere fraction of the size of those homes. Much of the contents of those boxes included information associated with her past and her upbringing. It took some time for me to sort through it all, but I was happy to do so.

And that was when I found it.

It was tucked away with Col. Holmes' Civil War diary. I had not seen it before; and had it not been specially bound in leather with marbled end papers and a ribbed spine, might easily have been discarded.

Kenesaw—that is what it read on the spine, spelled with just one "N." It was a different spelling from that which is now commonly used and considered correct: Kennesaw. It would be another seven years, however—exactly one hundred years after it was typewritten in 1915—before I would sit down by the fireplace to read it and find out what it was all about.

It was fascinating from the start. An easy read, it contained hand-drawn sketches of the Battle of "Kenesaw" as he had seen it unfold, and I read it in its entirety before putting it down. It was history. It was one of a kind. It was compelling, and it presented a story and an argument which Col. J.T. Holmes felt needed to be told—but to whom? I was certain that no other copy existed. I believed that it was intended for someone who followed in his family, a descendant, and not for mass publication. It was meant for me.

Preface by Garth D. Bishop

Divine intervention? Perhaps. But while reading the book, I felt that Col. Holmes was speaking to me alone, and that he now wanted his story to be shared by others. I was convinced that I was to be the vehicle for the purpose.

Clutching the book in my hands, I could feel its historical significance and persuasive power. I feared that should the book be lost, stolen or become a victim to fire, its history would be gone forever. I suspected that it held what was left of a story which needed to be told to everyone, especially to those whose interest lay in the Civil War, and whose familiarity with it and the documentary of some of its battles, particularly "Kenesaw," could with an open mind be easily persuaded by its compelling content and arguments, and that perhaps previously written accounts of how the battle went down may, in many respects, be incorrect.

As with many who are fortunate enough to get up in age, a natural interest in their own ancestry and heritage begins to creep in and take hold. I was no exception. As Col. James Taylor Holmes' great-grandson, I felt a connection to him. Through his written words, I was sympathetic to his account of the battle at Kennesaw. And, on his behalf, I was determined to get his story out. I also was determined to learn more about Col. Holmes, the man. My research began, and I was fortunate to obtain some important information about him and his life.

Author Nixon B. Stewart wrote a historical account and summary of Col. Holmes in his book from the year 1900:

> Major J. Taylor Holmes was promoted to Major from Captain of Co. G, March 8, 1863, and was promoted to Lieutenant Colonel, January 31, 1865, but not mustered. He was mustered out with the regiment as Brevet Lieutenant Colonel. Major Holmes was a born gentleman, scholar and soldier. He was publicly and officially complimented for his bravery and efficiency in drill and tactics and was perhaps as well known as any other officer of equal rank in the 14th Corps, for his equestrian appearance on the march, or on the field of battle. Major Holmes, as we still call him, was captured at Lexington, Kentucky, while sick, and was a prisoner for three months. He was wounded while leading the Regiment at Jonesboro. He was mustered out with the regiment, entered the law practice, and lives in the city of Columbus, Ohio. By frugality and hard work, he is able to welcome a beautiful old age, which is slowly coming on. He is a loyal Christian soldier and frequently fills the pulpit of the Broad Street M.E. Church, of which he is an honored member. Comrades desiring to find him can call on, or address him, in the National Bank Building, South High Street, Columbus, Ohio.

Preface by Garth D. Bishop

I was afforded the opportunity to sort through an extensive scrapbook Col. J.T. Holmes compiled over the years after his service. It was well preserved, and contained letters to his parents and others that had been arranged chronologically.

In the scrapbook was a signed document, inserted by his son Lawrence Asa Holmes, a memorial tribute to his father (included in the appendix to this volume) that described the Colonel as "peerless in courage and in wisdom; as a comrade he was unfailing in sympathy, alert in assistance, a co-sufferer with his men in their every privation, always first in facing the foe, last in leaving the field."

The fourth paragraph begins with a sentence of great interest, for it describes my great-grandfather's general demeanor after the Civil War: "The private life of Colonel Holmes was one of peculiar loneliness, of great reticence, and of studious reserve."

And why not? When one notes the listed battles in which he participated, it is easy to submit that by all accounts, he saw a lot of death and destruction of and by his fellow Americans. And likely, as was typically noted of those brave soldiers who fought in World War II—our "greatest generation"—the ones who saw the most spoke about it the least. While Colonel Holmes may not have been inclined to discuss what he saw, we are fortunate that those horrific experiences did not inhibit or preclude his ability and desire to write about them. He had an insatiable desire for knowledge, and his thirst to have everything recorded was not easily quenched. Hours of his time went into the compilation and documentation of the clash now known as the Battle of Kennesaw Mountain, and we are fortunate to be able to read about them here as they are set forth and outlined in this book.

Col. James Taylor Holmes became a lawyer, and a good one, after the Civil War. His successful career enabled him to become a founder and a president of the Ohio State Bar Association. Working out of Columbus, he amassed the largest law library in the state. I learned quickly that Col. J.T. Holmes was a very smart man.

The way he wrote, the way he thought, his ability to put into words what he saw on the battlefield reflects a man of high intellect, and it is easy to see that he was a master of the English language. No editing of his account of the battle was necessary, and I give you an intriguing example

Preface by Garth D. Bishop

Col. Holmes and "Jocko," ca. 1865 (family archives).

from a book which he authored, *Then and Now* (1915), whereupon he revisited the Kennesaw battlefield, and Cheatham Hill in particular, some 33 years after that fateful day of June 27, 1864, when he wrote a simple three word summary in his battlefield diary: "It was terrible."

> We walked about over the hill side within our works. Mr. Channel* called special attention to a little, stunted, gnarled oak, fifteen or twenty feet high and from four to six inches in diameter which was literally shot to pieces during the battle. It stands in the present edge of the timber just back of our position and had been shot through and through, I was about to say, hundreds of times. No man can tell how often. The tree has not grown in size since the war. It must have had some defect in one side at the time of the action; at least, it shows it now, for the bullets made openings through the tree in several places and the splinters and frayed edges of the wood are there still only slightly modified by time. Mr. Channell said that not long—a year or two—ago, a captain of one of the Illinois regiments in his presence, put his finger into one of these holes and pulled out a bullet which had lodged there during the battle. A boy Mr. C. had working for him, last year, not appreciating the character of the relic, proceeded to chop the tree down. The farmer happened to note what was going on in time to save it. The fresh ax marks

Preface by Garth D. Bishop

are at the root, however. The struggle of the tree for life excited curiosity and interest. It had been wounded almost to death and through the third of a century had barely lived. Some little repair of the ravages of war has taken place which looks like the healing or partial healing over of the wounds, yet so great has been the struggle to live that the remaining vitality has been more than consumed in the effort to heal and no other growth beyond the few leaves each year has occurred. It reminded me of many a poor fellow who went home with wounds and scars to drag out a miserable existence, never well, never strong, ever living and yet ever dying, until the end came, or will come, as come it must to the little oak of Kenesaw. Here, as at Chickamauga, the timber shows its scars all over, but one who has not studied effects would not comprehend or appreciate what the small or larger gnarled growths mean.

In all the destruction of time by artillery which I ever saw, that along the Lafayette road in the vicinity of the Kelly house took the lead. While I passed over that road many times in the first four months of 1864, and while the riven, mangled trees showed white, fresh wounds the interest never abated. It was a horrid dream, a bloody drama, a patch of hell on earth, and it came back with each new sight of the terrific indices of the dread actualities, which had been hung up on the forest trees along that Chickamauga thoroughfare.

Mr. Virgil B. Channel was the current owner of the land upon which the Kenesaw battle took place. Cheatham Hill was the name given to the hill up which we charged on that hot June day. General Frank Cheatham, of Nashville, who died September 4, 1886, commanded that portion of the Confederate lines and his name very appropriately sticks, as did his troops, to the hill.

My great-grandfather rode a famous horse during the Civil War. He was purchased from U.S. Col. Joseph Jackson Woods and was completely white when foaled in the fall of 1861, with marks of an Arabian and a Mexican bronco. Woods had bought him from a Mississippi planter, who had bought it from a Comanche. He was the only horse to survive the Carolinas campaign, and the March to the Sea.

According to Colonel Holmes, "Jack" was "the best piece of horseflesh, according to size, that I ever saw. His strength, endurance and intelligence were marvelous." His name then was plain Jack, but in time was metamorphosed, by others, into Jocko.

Jocko stood out as much on the battlefield as did his rider. He died September 22, 1892, having accidentally broken his leg on the Alum Creek, Franklin County, Ohio, farm of W.T. Rees, and had to be put down as a result.

Colonel Holmes felt that since Jocko had broken his leg while elderly, yet still active, the injury qualified as one endured in the heat of battle,

Preface by Garth D. Bishop

"while his boots were on." Similarly, and appropriately, since Jocko was buried on the banks of the Alum Creek by a former soldier, the burial was rightfully given "full military honors."

Colonel Holmes was wounded in the battle at Jonesboro, Georgia, on September 1, 1864. By his account in *Then and Now*:

> The guns were working on us and my men were trailing arms, making double quick time toward the battery. A shell exploded just as it left one of the guns and a fragment, the size of a man's hand, struck my left knee with disabling force. It was about seventy yards from the battery to the point where I fell alongside of the little bush margined gorge or ravine. At the instant, I called to Captain Hutchison to take command of the regiment, but I was in error as Captain Rothacker ranked him. They corrected the error and the line swept up to the battery and was in at its capture. The men immediately turned the pieces and began firing at the retreating enemy. There was a quantity of loose powder and unexploded shells lying about and presently one of the guns by its flash ignited the powder and an explosion followed, which killed and injured several of the men. Among the former was Robert N. Mercer of Company B, who was horribly burned in the explosion. Mercer was a short, stout young fellow, remarkable for the size of the knapsack, which he always carried and for his faithful, staying qualities as a soldier. He was quiet, patient, dutiful, and never known to complain or grumble at any demand made on him for any duty as a soldier.
>
> When I fell from the blow of the fragment of shell, I was assisted out of the way of the men and into the scant shelter of a tall stump which stood six or eight feet away.
>
> Michael Madden of Company K stopped beside me, having caught me as I reeled, and, as soon as the circulation began to relieve the numbness in my left leg, he supported me back to the knoll from which we had started on the charge. Minies were still flying when we started back, but after [a]while the night came on and the defeated rebels, being pushed back, were too far off for effective work, or ceased firing. I was in the field hospital that night and part of the next day, but moved with the regiment, though obliged for a whole month to mount my horse from the right side, which was the wrong side, because I could not bend the left knee to put that foot in the stirrup.

I am grateful to my great-grandfather for having the desire to write this book. It was first and foremost a self-serving treatise, borne out of the frustration he felt in 1914 when an Illinois monument was erected at the Kennesaw battlefield. I am certain that he suspected a descendant would eventually find it, read it, appreciate what he had to say, and take up his argument publicly, as I have done here, more than 100 years after his passing in 1916.

Preface by Garth D. Bishop

Time tends to distort the facts, but he was certain of his historical account of the Battle of Kennesaw Mountain as it is written here; he adamantly insisted that it would stand the test of time. And while he credited any and all soldiers who fought for the Union as brave and honorable, there is no room for those who sought benefits from its revision, as 50 years of passing time may and did allow; and that hyperbole and distortion of these facts and accounts, for their own selfish endeavors, borders on heresy, treason and blasphemy. I trust that he was certain the book and the story, should it be found, read, saved and told, would eventually set the record straight, and stand the test of time, as books do.

It is hard to disagree with famed author Clarence Day, who achieved lasting fame in literary circles for his comment:

> The world of books is the most remarkable creation of man. Nothing else that he builds ever lasts. Monuments fall, nations perish, civilizations grow old and die out; and, after an era of darkness, new races build others. But in the world of books are volumes that have seen this happen again and again, and yet live on, still young, still as fresh as the day they were written, still telling men's hearts of the hearts of men centuries dead.

Colonel Holmes would have agreed with Clarence Day.

As the editor of this book, my dedication to my great-grandfather is somewhat of an anomaly, for these are his own words, his thoughts, his accounts, his opinions, not my own. The dedication therefore is to duly honor him, and to thank him for having taken the time to record his thoughts and actions, and to set the record straight, enabling all readers to enjoy its particularly unique insight and perspective.

Read this book and be entertained by Col. Holmes' words; enjoy the ease in which he enables the reader to visualize the scenes; feel the sense of presence that his battlefield descriptions evoke. Sympathize with his desire to keep the records of history accurate and intact; and decipher if Col. Holmes has won the case for change of some of the current historical accounts of those who were also there, yet for apparently selfish reasons, summarized their accounts differently in an effort to achieve historical immortality.

Introduction

BY MARK A. SMITH

James Taylor Holmes's early twentieth-century memoir of the battle at Kennesaw Mountain, published here for the first time, sheds new light on Union military operations at Cheatham's Hill in late June and early July 1864, while simultaneously reminding us that history is malleable. In this work, Holmes focused less on his own personal actions and more on those of his regiment and, to a lesser extent, his brigade, and as a consequence, his work refines our understanding of some of the tactical aspects of the Federal attack against the Kennesaw Line and the brief stalemate that followed. He also connected those battlefield events with the steps taken to celebrate them and their participants a half-century later, commemorations that have shaped and, Holmes might have suggested, warped our subsequent understanding of them. His discussion of the battle and its memorialization is a reminder that our view of the past is crafted by individuals who are fallible beings, and that as a result history is always susceptible to revision. This reminder seems particularly timely in 2018 as our society continues to debate the meanings of the Civil War and its late-nineteenth and early-twentieth century monuments.

* * *

Holmes was born on November 25, 1837, to Asa and Mary McCoy Holmes of Short Creek, Ohio. Asa was a farmer, and James was the first of five boys and five girls that he and Mary raised. As a youth, James attended the public schools of eastern Ohio in Harrison County, receiving an education that prepared him well for further studies. He completed

Introduction by Mark A. Smith

the classical curriculum of Franklin College in New Athens, Ohio, in only three years, graduating in 1859.[1]

By the end of that year, Holmes had accepted the presidency of Richmond College. He moved into the boarding house run by John and Sarah Wagoner in the Ohio town of Richmond, and he served as the college's president until July 1862. Elected to the chair of mathematics at Iowa Wesleyan University that summer, Holmes seemed well on his way to an academic career. He declined the proffered position in Iowa, however, and shortly thereafter he also resigned the presidency of Richmond College so he could join the Union military.[2]

In early August, Holmes secured a commission from Ohio Governor David Tod as a lieutenant in a new Buckeye unit, the 52nd Ohio Volunteer Infantry. This position was contingent upon Holmes's successful recruitment of a company, which he accomplished in about a week. His company, which included his younger brother Abraham as its sergeant, promptly elected the elder Holmes its captain and was mustered in as Company G of the 52nd Ohio that same month. The regiment itself was commanded by Colonel Daniel McCook Jr., of the famous "fighting McCooks," which included Dan, as the 52nd's colonel was known familiarly, his father Daniel Sr., nine brothers, his uncle John, and five cousins, all of whom served in the Union military in some capacity.[3]

J.T. Holmes, captain and major of Company G, 52nd Ohio Volunteer Infantry (*Re-Union of Col. Dan McCook's Third Brigade, 1900*, p. 86).

Introduction by Mark A. Smith

Once mustered in at Camp Denison, the new regiment was almost immediately called into service. Before the end of August, the 52nd Ohio was dispatched to Lexington, Kentucky, to assist Federal forces under Major General William Nelson, who had been defeated by Edmund Kirby Smith's Confederates. By dawn on the last day of the month, McCook's regiment was with Union forces at the Kentucky River fifteen miles south of Lexington when Kirby Smith's rebels drove the Federals back toward the town during a severe rainstorm. Captain Holmes caught a fever on this retreat and was inadvertently left behind in Lexington when the Federals withdrew toward Louisville the next day. When Kirby Smith's Confederates took Lexington on September 2, they made Holmes a prisoner. He was paroled almost immediately, but he sat out the next three months of the war at Camp Chase and Camp Lew Wallace where he awaited exchange.[4]

Daniel McCook, Jr., was colonel of the 52nd Ohio, though shortly after its organization he was elevated to command a newly organized brigade that included the 52nd (Library of Congress).

While Holmes was sidelined, his regiment continued the retreat to Louisville where Federal forces were reorganized under Major General Don Carlos Buell in late September 1862. It was here that the 52nd Ohio was brigaded with three Illinois units with which it retained lasting connections: the 85th, 86th, and 125th volunteer regiments. Despite the preponderance of Illinoisans, Colonel McCook from the one Buckeye regiment was put in overall command of the new brigade. While this newly-organized unit changed divisions and, consequently, numbers over

Introduction by Mark A. Smith

the ensuing months, the brigade remained more or less intact, and its original four regiments served together from the fall of 1862 until the end of the war, though other units were subsequently attached to it. Beginning at Perryville in October, Battery I of the 2nd Illinois Light Artillery often served with it and was later included in its postwar reunions, and in early 1864, the 22nd Indiana was also added to the brigade.[5]

Captain Holmes was exchanged in mid–December 1862, and after gathering up the other exchanged men from his regiment he led them back to the 52nd, having missed the battle of Perryville, in which his unit participated, and the battle of Stones River, which the 52nd had sat out as part of the Nashville garrison. Holmes rejoined the unit in that city, then occupied by Union troops under Major General William S. Rosecrans.[6]

From January 1863 until the end of the war, Holmes remained on duty with his regiment. During the Tullahoma campaign in the early summer of 1863, while Rosecrans maneuvered Braxton Bragg's Confederate army out of middle Tennessee to Chattanooga, the 52nd Ohio was part of the garrison of Murfreesboro. By this time, Holmes was a major; in May he had been promoted over more senior captains at Colonel McCook's request so that Holmes could command the regiment during the absence of its ailing lieutenant colonel.[7] When Rosecrans moved from Murfreesboro against Bragg later that summer, maneuvering the rebels out of Chattanooga, the 52nd Ohio left Nashville for Bridgeport in extreme northeastern Ala-

Major General Jefferson C. Davis commanded the Second Division, XIV Corps, Army of the Cumberland throughout most of the Atlanta Campaign. Holmes's 52nd Ohio was part of the division's Third Brigade (Library of Congress).

Introduction by Mark A. Smith

bama as part of the Reserve Corps under Major General Gordon Granger. Early on this march, the brigade passed through Lynnville in south central Tennessee where it was fired on by southern partisans, leading McCook to destroy several homes in the town in retaliation. A few days beyond Lynnville, the brigade also passed by the home of the Alabama guerrilla, Frank Gurley, who had murdered Colonel McCook's older brother, Brigadier General Robert L. McCook, a year earlier. On the colonel's order, the 52nd Ohio destroyed Gurley's home before continuing on to Bridgeport. From there, the brigade moved on to Chattanooga and then joined the main Union army at Rossville Gap in northwestern Georgia.[8]

At the battle of Chickamauga where Braxton Bragg turned on Rosecrans's Federal Army of the Cumberland that was pursuing him into northern Georgia, the 52nd Ohio, led by Major Holmes, accompanied McCook's brigade to the Union left. There, on the afternoon of September 18, McCook and his men joined Colonel Robert Minty's cavalry brigade, which was guarding Reed's Bridge over Chickamauga Creek. Early the next morning, after McCook had been ordered to rejoin the Reserve Corps farther north, his men opened the day's fighting by skirmishing with the 6th Georgia Cavalry while filling their canteens from a nearby spring. This was their only contribution to the battle's first day; they spent the rest of it at Rossville and Ringgold as part of Rosecrans's reserves.[9]

On the second day of Chickamauga, September 20, McCook's brigade remained with Granger's Reserve Corps at McAfee's Church, two miles north of the battlefield on the Union left. It stayed there while James Longstreet launched the Confederate assault that struck a gap in the Federal lines on Rosecrans's right and sent a third of the Union army into a pell-mell retreat for Chattanooga. While George H. Thomas held firm on the Union left that afternoon, Granger advanced two brigades on his own authority to support Thomas, leaving McCook's to cover the road north to Ringgold from a small hill. The brigade came under rebel artillery fire as it moved into this position, but once firmly ensconced on the hill, the fire did the men little harm. They stayed there until after dark when Thomas successfully disengaged what was left of the Army of the Cumberland and headed north to Chattanooga. McCook's brigade, which had played little role in the day's fighting, was the last to leave the battlefield.[10]

Introduction by Mark A. Smith

At Chattanooga, McCook's men spent most of the ensuing siege camped at the mouth of North Chickamauga Creek on the north bank of the Tennessee River, northeast of the city. The brigade, including Major Holmes and the 52nd Ohio, was at this camp when George Thomas replaced Rosecrans at the head of the Army of the Cumberland in late October, and it was still there when it found a permanent organizational home, becoming the Third Brigade of Brigadier General Jefferson C. Davis's Second Division of the XIV Corps. During these developments, food and supplies became increasingly scarce because rebel guns commanded the approaches to the city after Bragg's Confederates took position on Lookout Mountain southwest of Chattanooga and on Missionary Ridge to the southeast. Two of McCook's regiments, the 52nd Ohio and the 86th Illinois, helped solved this problem. Shortly after he arrived to command all Union forces in Chattanooga, Major General Ulysses S. Grant implemented a plan to open the so-called "Cracker Line" to bring in supplies from Brown's Ferry west of the city. The 52nd and 86th went to help Joseph Hooker's XX Corps open this route by guarding some of the gaps in the low hills around the western base of Lookout Mountain. For a week, the two regiments were on duty almost constantly, in poor weather, and under daily bombardment by rebel batteries.[11]

Once the new supply line was open, Grant began planning operations to drive Bragg's Confederates out of their mountain stronghold and open the way for a Union invasion of Georgia. His forces in Chattanooga consisted of Thomas's Army of the Cumberland, Hooker's corps from the Army of the Potomac, and Major General William T. Sherman with the Army of the Tennessee. Grant attacked both rebel flanks below Chattanooga; Hooker's men hit the western flank, and Sherman's moved against the eastern one, while Thomas held the center. But McCook's Third Brigade, along with the rest of Jefferson C. Davis's division from Thomas's army, supported Sherman's late–November assault on the Confederate right. As a result, Holmes and his comrades did not join the Army of the Cumberland's unplanned attack on the center of Bragg's line atop Missionary Ridge which drove the rebels into a precipitous retreat into North Georgia.[12]

Once Chattanooga was secure, Grant dispatched Sherman's Army of the Tennessee to Knoxville to relieve Ambrose Burnside, who was besieged

Introduction by Mark A. Smith

in that city by James Longstreet. Temporarily attached to Sherman's army were the XI and XIV corps, the latter including Colonel McCook's brigade and the 52nd Ohio. Burnside, however, extricated himself, and though Sherman visited him briefly in Knoxville, not all of his soldiers did. The 52nd Ohio and the rest of its brigade stopped short of the city and returned to Chattanooga. A few days later, it relocated to McAfee's Church just north of the Tennessee-Georgia line, where it camped for two and a half months. Here, in early 1864, the 22nd Indiana joined the Third Brigade, giving it its final regimental structure just before the unit moved to Lee and Gordon's Mills on Chickamauga Creek. At this new camp, Major Holmes developed and implemented his own unique system of drill during the winter of 1863–1864, earning him a minor reputation as an excellent troop handler. Lee and Gordon's Mills was also where the brigade started the campaign for Atlanta under Sherman in the spring of 1864.[13]

Sherman maneuvered Bragg's replacement, Joseph E. Johnston, south through northern Georgia with only a few major engagements, including one at Kennesaw Mountain that is examined more minutely below and that cost Colonel McCook his life. Johnston's repeated withdrawals, however, prompted the Confederate president to replace him with John Bell Hood just north of Atlanta. When he took command, Hood undermined the Confederate Army of Tennessee's offensive capabilities in a series of unwise assaults and then withdrew into the prepared defenses of Atlanta. Sherman slowly surrounded the city, cutting off all its rail lines; he severed the last of them following the battle of Jonesboro on September 1. Major Holmes was wounded slightly in this fight by a rebel shell fragment that struck him in the knee as he led the 52nd Ohio. He remained with his regiment, however, participating in the occupation of the Atlanta that began the day after the battle at Jonesboro.[14]

During the occupation, the 52nd Ohio camped along Whitehall Street just south of the city center. It stayed there for most of September with the rest of Davis's division. On the twenty-ninth, though, the brigade moved north with the Army of the Cumberland and spent the next several weeks trying to clear Nathan Bedford Forrest's Confederate cavalry out of northern Alabama and southern Tennessee where it threatened Sherman's supply line.[15]

Introduction by Mark A. Smith

McCook's former brigade, however, did not join Thomas in late 1864 when Sherman sent him to destroy Hood's Confederate army in Tennessee; instead, the Third Brigade returned to Atlanta in mid–November where it, along with the entire XIV Corps, became part of the newly-formed Army of Georgia under Major General Henry Slocum. As a part of this new organization, the brigade accompanied Sherman on his famous marches through Georgia and the Carolinas in late 1864 and early 1865. At Bentonville, the brigade, now led by Brigadier General Benjamin D. Fearing, participated in the critical Union stand made by the Second Division of the XIV Corps when it was attacked simultaneously from the front, the left, and the rear by Confederate forces once again commanded by Joseph Johnston. The brigade and its division held their ground, and after a few more days of skirmishing, Johnston withdrew. Within a month of that engagement, Union victory was secured, and by the end of April Sherman's army was marching for Washington. Following the Grand Review in the capital, the 52nd Ohio was mustered out on June 3, 1865, after which Major Holmes led its men back to the Buckeye State.[16]

By the middle of June 1865, James Holmes's war was over, and he set about building a peacetime life for himself. Starting that summer, he studied under a lawyer in Columbus, Ohio, and within two years he was admitted to the bar. After a trip out west to visit the Great Plains, he opened his own law practice in Columbus in early 1868. By all accounts he was well-respected within the profession. In 1880 he helped found the Ohio State Bar Association, serving as its secretary for a decade before being elected its president in 1890.[17] Holmes also started a family. On December 28, 1871, he married Lucy K. Bates, twelve years his junior. Together they had five children, four of whom survived to adulthood. Three daughters and a son all grew up in Columbus, and Holmes himself died there in early 1916, just a few months after dictating the memoir presented here. He was buried in Green Lawn Cemetery.[18]

Despite its conclusion more than a half-century prior to his death, Holmes always remembered his military service on behalf of the Union. In 1897, he and Lucy retraced the route of his campaigns in a trip that served as the basis for *52d O.V.I.: Then and Now*, Holmes's privately printed 1898 work that was both a memoir of his wartime experiences

Introduction by Mark A. Smith

and a travelogue detailing this late-nineteenth century trip with his wife. What seems to have stood out most vividly to him was the Atlanta Campaign and the crucial part played in it by his regiment and its brigade at the battle of Kennesaw Mountain (spelled "Kenesaw" during the war). It was this battle and its immediate aftermath, as well as attempts to record and memorialize these events long after the fact, that prompted Holmes to write his two-part early twentieth-century memoir on Kennesaw. To fully grasp the import of his recollections, however, a more complete understanding of the engagement and the campaign is required.

* * *

In May 1864, Major General William Tecumseh Sherman opened his Atlanta Campaign with over 98,000 men divided among three separate Federal armies. With 13,500 men, the Army of the Ohio under Major General John M. Schofield was the smallest; next in size was Major General James McPherson's 24,400-man Army of the Tennessee. The largest, which included the 52nd Ohio and Major James Holmes, was the Army of the Cumberland, whose 60,700 men were led by Major General George H. Thomas. Sherman had concentrated all these forces around Chattanooga by early May 1864 in preparation for his upcoming campaign. His objective was the Confederate Army of Tennessee under General Joseph E. Johnston.[19]

Major General George H. Thomas commanded the Army of the Cumberland throughout the Atlanta Campaign (Library of Congress).

Introduction by Mark A. Smith

Johnston started with about 60,000 men effectively divided into three corps that were led by William J. Hardee, John Bell Hood, and Leonidas Polk, though Polk actually commanded the corps-sized Army of Mississippi. As the opposing forces moved south, however, Confederate numbers increased because the rebels approached their base at Atlanta and shortened their supply lines. Sherman's effective force, however, only declined as the campaign proceeded and took him farther from his advanced base at Chattanooga, forcing him to detach men to guard his lines of communication and supply. When the campaign opened, however, Johnston posted his men on Rocky Face Ridge in front of Dalton, Georgia, where they commanded the Western and Atlantic Railroad, a single-track line that connected Johnston with his base to the south and also linked Sherman with his base to the north.[20]

Sherman had no intention of assaulting Johnston's line on Rocky Face Ridge to secure the railroad. Instead, he adopted an approach he used throughout most of the campaign; he tried to turn the Confederate left, threatening Johnston's line of communications. Faced with this threat, Johnston usually retreated. At the opening of the campaign, Johnston had neglected the defense of Snake Creek Gap, a pass through the mountains a dozen miles south of Dalton. Sherman sent McPherson's Army of the Tennessee through that gap toward the Western and Atlantic while Thomas and Schofield held Johnston's attention in front of Dalton. McPherson, however, let two Confederate brigades stop him short of the railroad. Nevertheless once Johnston became aware of McPherson's movement, he retreated fifteen miles south to Resaca on May 12.[21]

Sherman's blue-clad soldiers followed the retreating rebels the next day and came upon them in a fortified line behind Camp Creek north and west of Resaca. During a series of Union attacks against this main rebel line on the fourteenth, McPherson crossed the Oostanaula River at Lay's Ferry a few miles south of the town, once again imperiling the rebel line of communication. Johnston recognized this danger on the afternoon of May 15, and he pulled back across the Oostanaula that night.[22] Following a brief stopover at Adairsville, the Confederate Army of Tennessee withdrew to Cassville where it was in position by the eighteenth. As the Union forces arrived the next day and Johnston adjusted his position, a flaw developed in the rebel lines that allowed Federal artillery to enfilade a

Introduction by Mark A. Smith

point in the Confederate center. The next day, Johnston withdrew again, this time at the urging of his two corps commanders, Polk and Hood. From Cassville, the rebels moved south of the Etowah River, and Sherman paused for a few days to rest his men, bring forward supplies, and repair the bridges over the river.[23]

Part of the reason for this Union delay was that Sherman planned to temporarily abandon his railroad supply line when he crossed the Etowah. As a consequence, the Federal commander needed time to collect the supplies his armies would require while relying on wagon transport. He planned to avoid the Allatoona Hills along the railroad line south of the Etowah River by moving his entire force west, away from the Western and Atlantic and towards Dallas. This small crossroads village was about fifteen miles south of the Etowah and a similar distance west of Marietta, through which the railroad ran before crossing the Chattahoochee River another dozen or so miles to the south. Sherman expected these movements to prompt Johnston to withdraw south to Marietta or even to the south bank of the Chattahoochee without a fight. In this, though, the Union general was disappointed.[24]

The Federal armies began crossing the Etowah on May 23, heading for Dallas, but Johnston learned of the Union crossings that very morning and deduced their objective. He sent Polk's and Hardee's corps to block the Federal advance. The latter succeeded at New Hope Church, a Methodist meeting-house northeast of Dallas where the XX Corps under Joseph Hooker was halted by Hardee's men after a sharp fight on the afternoon of the twenty-fifth. Both sides dug in afterwards, and skirmishing continued the next day as they developed their positions. On May 27, Sherman tried and failed to drive back both rebel flanks. McPherson, on the Union right, found his progress blocked by strong Confederate entrenchments, while on the Federal left, the IV Corps of Oliver Otis Howard was repulsed near Pickett's Mill. After these failures, the Union commander shortened the arc of his westward flanking movement and opted for an early return to his railroad supply line around Allatoona, which Johnston had abandoned when the Federals moved toward Dallas. Once they repelled a May 28 Confederate assault near that village on the Union right, the Federals began the slow process of shifting east toward the railroad. On June 4, two days after the start of a steady rain, Johnston

Introduction by Mark A. Smith

abandoned his line from Dallas to Pickett's Mill. He moved east to take a position covering the railroad above Marietta from Lost Mountain in the east to Brush Mountain in the west. This rebel movement let Sherman advance to Acworth on the Western and Atlantic, where his men arrived on June 6.[25]

On June 10, Sherman shifted to Big Shanty on the railroad as the rain continued to fall. From there, his men cautiously approached the new Confederate line between Lost and Brush mountains. On the fourteenth, as the rain began to let up, Sherman reconnoitered this new line, ordering some of his artillery to disperse a gathering of rebels on Pine Mountain, an advanced outpost in front of the rebel center. The resulting fire killed Confederate General Leonidas Polk, and William W. Loring took his place in Johnston's army. Sherman ordered Thomas's Army of the Cumberland to break the rebel line near Pine Mountain the next day, but Johnston abandoned this advanced position that night and Thomas's assault became a reconnaissance-in-force that stopped when it encountered the new rebel line through Gilgal Church between Lost and Brush mountains. The Union commander maintained pressure on the Confederate position at Gilgal Church on the sixteenth, with Holmes's regiment supporting the Union skirmish line in the Army of the Cumberland's movements. This Federal pressure convinced Johnston to abandon Gilgal Church and Lost Mountain to the west that very night. First, the rebel general moved east to a line behind Mud Creek, which flowed almost due south from Pine Mountain, but as Thomas again pursued cautiously for the Federals, Johnston was preparing an even more formidable line farther east, closer to Marietta. A heavy ran on the eighteenth impeded all maneuvers that day and gave Johnston the chance to complete this new position. That night the rebels withdrew to the Kennesaw Line.[26]

By the next morning, the Confederate Army of Tennessee held a formidable position seven miles long, running roughly north to south. Loring's Army of Mississippi held the center, including the heights west and south of the railroad. Big Kennesaw, nearly seven hundred feet high, was nearest the tracks on the Confederate right center; just southwest of it was Little Kennesaw with a height of about four hundred feet. Between Little Kennesaw and the Burnt Hickory Road to the south was another rise that was half as tall as the smaller Kennesaw and that was named

Introduction by Mark A. Smith

Pigeon Hill in the early twentieth century. Loring's men defended all of these plus the ground from Pigeon Hill and the Burnt Hickory Road south almost to the Dallas Road. In the north on Loring's right, Hood's corps curved back to the east to cover the rail line and Marietta, extending beyond the Bells Ferry and Canton roads. Hardee was on Loring's left, stretching south from just above the Dallas Road to John Ward Creek. As Sherman's Federals approached this position on the nineteenth, however, Johnston feared that the rain-swollen Noyes Creek, which turned south and ran in front of his left after crossing the center of his line, would provide a shield behind which Union forces could extend their lines and turn the rebel left. To counter this threat, the Confederate leader had Loring thin his lines and extend his right north beyond the railroad, and he placed Joseph Wheeler's Cavalry Corps on Loring's Right so he could shift Hood's corps south of Hardee's to extend the Confederate left. Hardee's move did not begin until the morning of June 21.[27]

As the rain continued on the twentieth and twenty-first, the two opponents jockeyed for position and dueled with their artillery. On the Union side, McPherson's Army of the Tennessee advanced along the Western and Atlantic, guarding the Federal supply line. Thomas held the center with his Army of the Cumberland. Schofield's Army of the Ohio came in on the Federal right, south of Thomas. On June 22, with the first dry weather in nearly three weeks, Sherman moved his right closer to Marietta, with Joseph Hooker's XX Corps, by now integrated into Thomas's army, driving northeast up the Powder Springs Road and Schofield advancing in the same direction farther south. That afternoon, Hooker ran into elements of Hood's Confederate corps, by then on the rebel left, and the Union corps commander started to prepare his men for a defensive battle near the farmhouse of Mrs. Kolb. Without informing Johnston, Hood attacked Hooker's line around 5 p.m with two divisions and very little preparation, leading to a handy repulse by Hooker's veterans.[28]

The day after the battle at Kolb's Farm, as the roads continued to dry out, Sherman had Schofield examine the possibility of turning the Confederates out of the Kennesaw Line by getting around their left. That evening, however, the Army of the Ohio commander reported that the rebel left actually extended beyond the Union right. With a successful turning

Introduction by Mark A. Smith

movement unlikely, that only left a direct assault as an option, but skirmishing on Thomas's front that day had convinced the Army of the Cumberland commander that he was facing formidable works. Sherman, however, was frustrated with the slow progress of his forces since early June, and on the twenty-fourth he opted to attack the Kennesaw Line near its center, hoping to break through and capture the railroad somewhere near Marietta, cutting Johnston's army in two.[29]

The Union general's plan called for two major assaults on June 27 and a diversion all along the line. Schofield was originally ordered to press forward near the Powder Springs Road, but these orders were altered before the battle, and instead he was directed to move one of his divisions south over Olley's Creek to threaten beyond the rebel left. At the other end of the line, McPherson was instructed to feint at the Confederate right while launching one of the two main attacks against Pigeon Hill and Little Kennesaw. Ultimately, however, McPherson's assault came to little except the expenditure of Union lives. Thomas's Army of the Cumberland was responsible for the other major effort, which was in the center and well south of McPherson's primary line of attack. Sherman allowed Thomas to select the precise locations of his assault, and Thomas gave the same freedom of choice to the commanders charged with making the attack. Oliver Howard of the IV Corps chose the line manned by Patrick Cleburne's Confederate division atop a small ridge that ran south from the Dallas Road. In particular, two of Howard's brigades led

Confederate Major General Benjamin F. Cheatham commanded the division that defended the rise on the rebel left at Kennesaw Mountain, a hill that was eventually named for him (Library of Congress).

22

Introduction by Mark A. Smith

Topographical versus military crest: hill "a" depicts the topographical or actual crest. Fire from this position will cover the area immediately around the crest of the hill, while the shaded area is not covered. Hill "b" shows the military crest of the same hill. Fire from this position will sweep the entire slope to the base (Mark A. Smith).

by George Wagner and Charles Harker were to strike the left of Cleburne's division where it joined with the rebel division commanded by Benjamin Franklin Cheatham. This allowed Howard's brigades, with Wagner on the left and Harker on the right, to cooperate with the two brigades of the Second Division, XIV Corps, slated to move forward farther south on their right. The unfortunately-named Union division commander, Jefferson C. Davis, chose the target for his two participating brigades, which were led by John G. Mitchell and Daniel McCook. Mitchell's men were to move forward on the extreme right of Thomas's assault, and to Mitchell's left, Dan McCook's brigade, including the 52nd Ohio and its major, James Holmes, would attack between Mitchell and Harker, aiming for a salient, or angle, in the Confederate line held by Cheatham's division.[30]

This salient was atop a small hill at the southern end of the ridge on which the Confederate line was located, and it was later known after its defender as Cheatham's Hill. It was a key feature of this part of the battlefield, and one that directly impacted the experiences of the men in McCook's Third Brigade. A salient, or protruding angle, is by itself a weakness in a defensive line because it exposes the men holding it to a simultaneous attack from two directions, though this particular angle was unavoidable given the local terrain. The ridge that the rebel defenses followed terminated at Cheatham's Hill; good defensive ground south of the hill was only available farther east, toward the Confederate rear. As a result, Cheatham's line had to turn sharply to the left at his eponymous hill in order to connect with the rebel positions to the south, thus creating the salient.[31]

Introduction by Mark A. Smith

Weakening this position even further, the works here were poorly sited by Confederate engineers. This poor location was related to the difference between the actual or topographical crest of a rise, and its *military* crest. The former is simply the highest point, but the latter is the highest location from which fire, either musketry or artillery, can sweep down the entire incline uninterrupted to its base. Any prominence with a slope that declines nearer to its actual crest creates a dead zone that fire from the topographical crest cannot sweep. In such a case, the military crest—the best position for a line from which to secure the hill against enemy assault—is sufficiently below the topographical crest to eliminate this dead zone and allow the defending force to fire down the entire rise of the hill below. At Cheatham's Hill, the Confederate engineers located the line too high, not quite on the actual crest but still above the military crest. The result was a dead zone about twenty-five to forty yards directly in front of the salient in the rebel position, beyond which the defenders could neither see nor direct their fire. Partly because of this dead zone and partly due to the enormous casualties the Union attacks against this site suffered, the poorly-located Confederate salient on Cheatham's Hill became known as the Dead Angle.[32]

Major General Cheatham discovered this flaw in his defenses on the hill at dawn on June 20, after having commenced this line the night before, but he decided to maintain the position and strengthen it as much as possible in the coming days. After a federal artillery bombardment on the twenty-third partly enfiladed, or fired parallel down, the southern part of the line at the salient, Cheatham put his men to work. They raised the parapet to a height of seven feet, added head logs to most of the line to cover the men as they fired over the parapet and beneath the head logs, built a firing step inside the main trench, and dug ditches toward the Confederate rear to provide additional shelter. The rebel division commander also advanced a force of skirmishers beyond this line, and while they could not secure the commanding heights across the valley from the salient, they did establish a line of rifle-pits at the base of the hill leading up to the Dead Angle. At the same time, however, a lack of large trees near the salient prevented the Confederate defenders there from erecting the same sort of exterior obstructions found immediately to their right, which included a heavy slashing of local timber as well as an abatis, a careful

Introduction by Mark A. Smith

arrangement of interlocking sharpened stakes that assailants had to halt and dismantle under fire. Instead, in front of the Dead Angle was what one historian calls "a flimsy pile of cut saplings."[33]

Charged with defending this position, and responsible for much of the work done to improve it, was Brigadier General George Maney's brigade of Cheatham's division. Left of the angle itself from the rebel perspective, and facing southwest, were the 19th, 4th, and 50th Tennessee regiments, followed by the 6th and 9th Tennessee (Consolidated) on the brigade's far left. On its right, defending the Dead Angle, was the 1st and 27th Tennessee (Consolidated) regiment; this unit's four right-most companies faced northwest from their position in the salient, while the other six faced south and southwest, connecting with the right of the 19th Tennesee. On Maney's right, north of the angle, Alfred Vaughan's brigade held the line, and south to Maney's left was John Carter's, both from Cheatham's division. Aware of the weakness of his line at the salient, Major General Cheatham also placed his artillery to establish a cross fire directly in front of the angle. He put eight guns just south of the salient on the right of Carter's brigade, and two north of it in Vaughan's line, all sited to create a cross fire and sweep the ground in front of the Dead Angle, though Cheatham kept these guns screened from enemy view prior to June 27.[34]

The Union soldiers who crossed this particular piece of deadly ground to attack the salient were members of Mitchell's Second Brigade and McCook's Third Brigade from Jefferson C. Davis's division of the XIV Corps. Davis had been serving as a reserve for McPherson's army in front of Pigeon Hill, but after dark on June 25, his division was relieved and marched south to a point behind David Stanley's division of the IV Corps, then opposite Cheatham's Hill. There Davis's men rested all day on the twenty-sixth. The two other brigades that participated in Thomas's June 27 assault, Harker's and Wagner's, belonged to John Newton's division of the IV Corps, but they did not move into position until the night of June 26–27, even though the attack was slated for 8 a.m. on the twenty-seventh.[35]

The men of these four brigades, plus those of Nathan Kimball's which supported Wagner's brigade in the IV Corps attack, were roused and fed before sunrise on June 27. About 6 a.m. that morning, they began to form

Introduction by Mark A. Smith

up for the impending assault. The two brigades from Davis's division of the XIV Corps, McCook's and Mitchell's, formed up just behind the main Union line, with Mitchell on the right and McCook to his left. Both brigades were arranged in a column of regiments, closed en masse. In this formation, each regiment was posted in a battle line two ranks deep, with about a foot and a half between the first and second rank; these regimental lines were then stacked one behind the other, with about twenty feet in between each separate regiment. Both McCook and Mitchell had four regiments in column, with a fifth one arrayed in front as skirmishers. Colonel McCook's brigade had the 85th Illinois out front as skirmishers; behind it, at about twenty-foot intervals, were the battle lines of the 125th Illinois, the 86th Illinois, the 22nd Indiana, and the 52nd Ohio, with its major, James T. Holmes. This arrangement gave the brigade a front the width of a regiment and a depth of about sixty feet, with four two-rank lines behind the skirmishers. It was the sort of heavy column recommended for assaulting a strongly-defended position, and in this arrangement, Mitchell and McCook would strike the weak point in the rebel lines defended by George Maney's Confederate brigade; Mitchell targeted the line just right of the salient and McCook aimed for the Dead Angle itself as well as portions of the rebel line north of it that were held by Vaughan's brigade.[36]

On McCook's left was Harker's brigade of the IV Corps; Wagner's brigade, supported by Kimball's, was to Harker's left. Despite their relatively close proximity, however, these units were not in direct contact with each other or with the XIV Corps brigades on their right because of their formations. Major General Howard had ordered them both to make their assaults in columns "with a regimental division front." A regimental division was two companies, and both columns on the IV Corps front adopted this narrowest of formations. Each regiment was arrayed in five two-company-wide battle lines and each regiment, thus arranged, lined up one behind the other, creating an extremely narrow but very deep formation. Harker's men were definitely organized in this formation, and it seems that Wagner's were, too, with Kimball's brigade arranged en echelon, or offset, to the left and rear of Wagner's brigade but still a part of its column. Because of their exceedingly narrow fronts, a hundred yards was left between the two IV Corps columns and between Harker and McCook, in

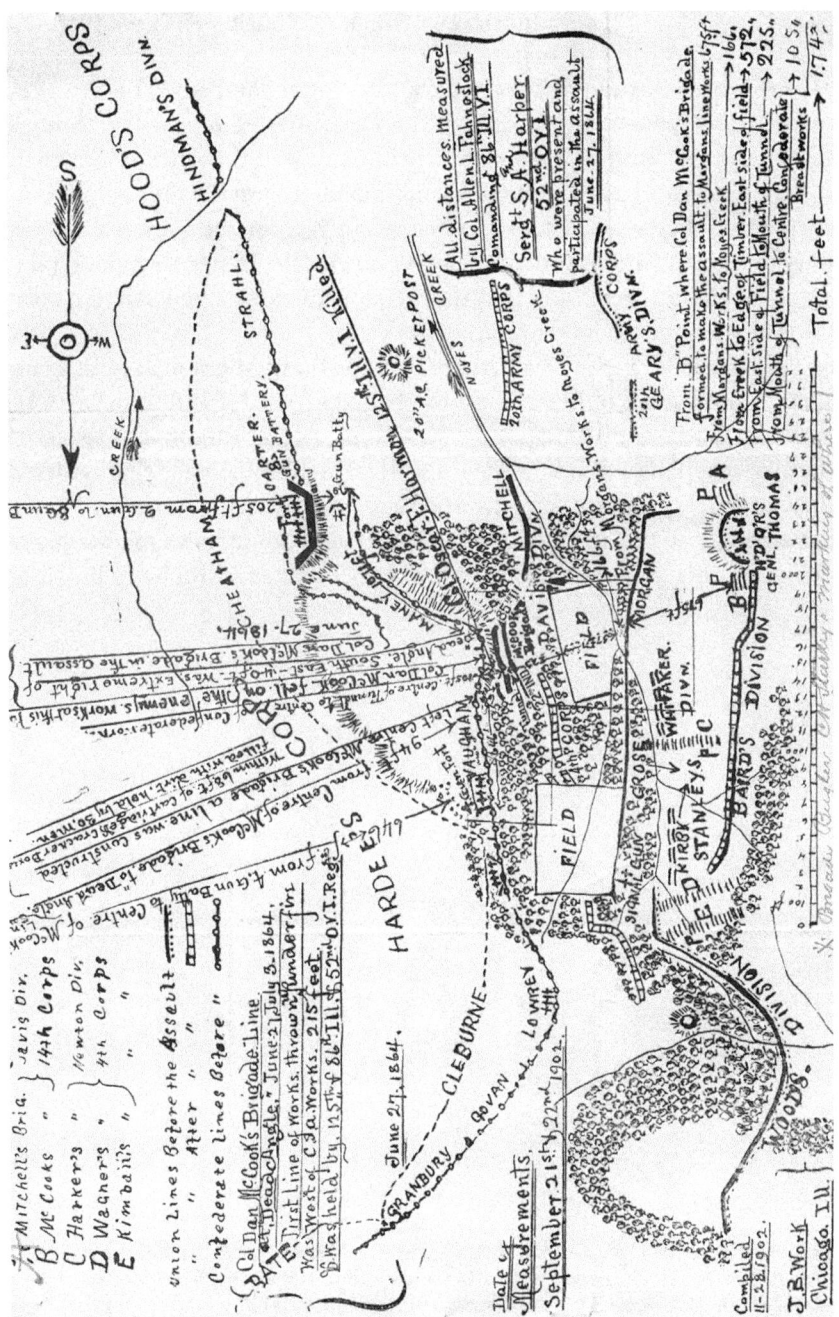

This map of the "Dead Angle," drawn by Julius B. Work in 1902, illustrates the portion of the battlefield where the brigades of the IV and XIV corps launched their attacks on June 27, 1864 (David M. Rubenstein Rare Book and Manuscripts Library, Duke University).

Introduction by Mark A. Smith

case the brigades needed to deploy into regimental lines before they reached the enemy works north of the Dead Angle. In practice, though, these gaps left both of Howard's brigades, as well as McCook's to their right, vulnerable to enfilading fire and unable to provide immediate support to one another. As a consequence, when Wagner and Harker assaulted the Confederate lines north of the rebel salient, they failed to make a lodgment, let alone a break, and they ultimately returned to their starting positions in something less than full order.[37]

Meanwhile, at the Dead Angle, McCook and Mitchell at least managed to hold some of the ground their men crossed. Sometime between 8:00 and 8:30 a.m., one of Thomas's artillery pieces fired a shot to signal the advance. This was followed by a Federal artillery barrage that targeted the Confederate entrenchments and that lasted until Union infantrymen came too close to the rebel line for the Federal gunners to maintain fire safely. As this bombardment opened, McCook's and Mitchell's brigades

The assault of Col. McCook's brigade on the "Dead Angle," Cheatham's Hill, June 27, 1864. McCook fell mortally wounded on the enemy's works (*Re-Union of Col. Dan McCook's Third Brigade, 1900*, frontispiece).

Introduction by Mark A. Smith

stepped off with bayonets fixed and orders not to fire until the Confederate breastworks were under Union control. The men moved down the slope at the quick time advancing behind and then across the forward Union line. At the bottom of the hill, about three hundred yards from their starting point, they crossed a small stream that was a branch of John Ward Creek, and as they crossed it, the Confederate artillery south of the Dead Angle began to fire. Crossing the stream briefly disorganized their formations, but the Union infantrymen quickly set their ranks straight and advanced across a meadow at the double-quick.[38]

As McCook's brigade reached the far side of the meadow, about two hundred yards from the creek and five hundred from its jumping off point, its men overran the Confederate skirmish line

Oscar F. Harmon began the assault at Kennesaw Mountain as colonel of the 125th Illinois. After McCook was mortally wounded, Harmon briefly assumed command of the Third Brigade before sustaining an injury that led to his death (*Re-Union of Col. Dan McCook's Third Brigade, 1900, p. 51*).

posted in a series of rifle-pits just inside a thick belt of woods. The Union skirmishers from the 85th Illinois seized their rebel counterparts. As some of these Hoosiers escorted the captured Confederate skirmishers to the rear, the rest continued to lead the brigade over the final hundred yards, through the trees and up the steeply rising slope towards Maney's and Vaughan's Confederates on Cheatham's Hill. As the Federals climbed upward, Confederate musketry and artillery fire both increased in volume, and the enemy's guns south of the salient began to enfilade the Federal column, firing down its length from the right. Simultaneously, the men of the 1st and 27th Tennessee poured their fire directly into the advancing

Introduction by Mark A. Smith

column while the rebel infantrymen to their left and right enfiladed it from both its flanks.[39]

Under the heavy rain of shot and shell, the only conceivable option for the blue-clad soldiers was to continue forward until the rebel gunners could no longer fire on the Federals without endangering their own men. As McCook's column approached the Tennessee volunteers behind the salient, however, the two Confederate guns to the north were finally unmasked and opened from close range. Under this withering fire, the 85th Illinois continued to lead the Third Brigade forward as skirmishers until nearly reaching the Confederate breastworks when its men fell back and joined the 125th Illinois at the front of the brigade's column for the initial Union assault against Cheatham's Hill. Colonel McCook, who had accompanied the 125th on foot, led this first attempt to take the Confederate line at the salient, even while his brigade's rearmost regiment, the 52nd Ohio, was still forty or sixty yards behind climbing up the steep slope. McCook was mortally wounded in the advance when a minie ball hit him in the chest, just below his right collarbone. He appears to have been standing near if not quite at the rebel parapet, perhaps some fifteen or twenty feet from the salient. Command of the brigade devolved upon Colonel Oscar F. Harmon of the 125th Illinois, but within five minutes he was killed almost instantly by a shot through the heart and the 85th's Colonel Caleb J. Dilworth took command of the

Colonel Caleb Dilworth led the 85th Illinois at the start of the Union assault on Cheatham's Hill. After the deaths of McCook and Harmon, Dilworth assumed command of the Third Brigade (*Re-Union of Col. Dan McCook's Third Brigade, 1900*, p. 50).

Introduction by Mark A. Smith

brigade. Meanwhile, the rest of the brigade's regiments came up. The 86th Illinois came behind the 125th, and the 22nd Indiana followed the 86th. Both made their own charges against Cheatham's Hill, each picking up a few men from the units that had preceded them. Finally the 52nd Ohio arrived in the best order of all the brigade's regiments, despite having passed through many of the walking wounded streaming the other way. The Ohioans, along with some of their comrades from other units, made one final attempt to take the hill. They could not take capture the position, but neither did they withdraw and risk exposing themselves to Confederate fire during a long retreat. Instead, they clung desperately to the ground just in front of the Confederate parapet.[40]

About twenty minutes after the brigade's first line struck the Confederate works, it became apparent that the men of the brigade could not remain so close to the rebel position indefinitely. Slowly, the men moved to the rear, taking advantage of whatever shelter they could find. But they did not go far. Indeed, the men on the brigade's right, immediately in front of the rebel salient, fell back only about twenty or thirty yards to the military crest of the hill, where its increasing

Shown here long after the war in civilian clothing, Lieutenant Colonel James W. Langley took command of the 125th Illinois on the afternoon of June 27. At the battle's beginning, Langley was serving on the staff of Major General John A. Palmer who commanded the XIV Corps. Once he learned of Harmon's death, Langley secured permission to join and lead his regiment. Toward the end of the Atlanta Campaign, just before the city's fall, he took command of the Third Brigade and subsequently authored its official report of the campaign (*Re-Union of Col. Dan McCook's Third Brigade, 1900, p. 100*).

Introduction by Mark A. Smith

downward slope provided just enough cover for a man lying prone. The men on the left and in the center, who had been stopped short of the main Confederate line by the obstructions in its front, also withdrew, though they had a greater distance to cover than the men on the right before reaching relative safety. By the time Colonel Dilworth ordered a retreat, it was already underway, but the men stopped at the military crest, and the officers disentangled the mixed regiments and restored some sort of order. Dilworth realized the value of the protection afforded by the ground, and he sent a subordinate to the rear to request entrenching tools. While awaiting a reply, he had about half his men maintain a covering fire while the other half advanced a few paces and scratched out a line of hasty field works with bayonets, plates, cups, and bare hands to provide some small protection for the men lying on the ground just a few short yards from the Confederate breastworks.[41]

In his definitive modern study of the battle at Kennesaw Mountain, Earl J. Hess reports that after it erected its hasty entrenchments on the morning of June 27, McCook's Third Brigade was arranged with the 22nd Indiana on the left, the 125th Illinois in the center, the 85th Illinois on the right, and both the 86th Illinois and 52nd Ohio "a short distance to the rear in reserve." His description of these regimental positions is based entirely on the report of Lieutenant Colonel James W. Langley, who commanded the brigade at the end of the Atlanta Cam-

Colonel Allen L. Fahnestock commanded the 86th Illinois during the Battle of Kennesaw Mountain (*Reunion of Col. Dan McCook's Third Brigade, 1900, p. 36*).

Introduction by Mark A. Smith

paign. None of the other reports or reminisces describe the relative positions of the brigade's units. Langley, however, was *not* with the brigade on the morning of June 27, and he did not join it until later in the afternoon after these initial works had been completed, though he asserted that the brigade's regiments were in the same position on the morning of June 28, by which time he was on the front line commanding the 125th Illinois. He wrote his brigade report in early September, however, based on the notes of Colonel Dilworth, who had been wounded at the battle of Jonesboro on September 1, just before the Atlanta Campaign ended. In the memoir that follows, James Holmes vehemently contested the assertion that the 52nd Ohio was ever in reserve, asserting instead that it held the center of the brigade's most advanced line from June 27 through July 3; these claims, however, become more relevant in regard to the brigade's actions after the initial assault, and they will be evaluated below in that context.[42]

While the Third Brigade struck Cheatham's Hill and pulled back a short distance before clinging tenaciously to a lightly-fortified position on the morning of June 27, Mitchell's Second Brigade, on its right, had a similar experience. Also attacking in a column of regiments, Mitchell planned to transform his column into a line of battle by having every regimental battle line move to the right when the unit in front of it struck the main Confederate position. As they approached the rebel works, though, his men encountered more obstructions than McCook's. As a result, most of Mitchell's men took what shelter they could find and opened fire well before reaching the rebel lines, leaving them more exposed to the enfilading artillery fire from their right. Eventually, Mitchell's soldiers also withdrew to the protection offered by the changing slope of the hill where they threw up their own light entrenchments that eventually connected with those of the Third Brigade on their left.[43]

By mid-morning the assault was over. Major General Davis's official statement of losses for his division during the assault listed 824 casualties, 414 of them from McCook's brigade, including 44 killed, 350 wounded, and 20 missing. Holmes's regiment, the 52nd Ohio, lost 108 men according to the report he filed at the end of the campaign. On June 27, though, many of the wounded and some who were just too close to the rebel trenches, were stuck between the lines until Union fire or darkness offered some cover. And some were so close to the Confederate works that they

Introduction by Mark A. Smith

could not make their way to the rear at all and could only surrender to Maney's Confederates.[44]

For the men in the shallow Union trenches, the rest of June 27 was consumed in trying to adjust their lines and improve their position, under Confederate fire, while returning fire. Despite Dilworth's request for entrenching tools earlier in the day, they did not arrive until almost dusk because General Thomas could not believe at first that Davis's two brigades were holding a position so close to the Confederate lines. Once the tools arrived, though, the men went to work with a will constructing a more permanent line of fortifications. The Third Brigade remained closest to the rebel works from its position just in front of the enemy salient, with both flanks refused and its right connected to the works of Mitchell's

The Illinois monument, unveiled and dedicated on the fiftieth anniversary of the Federal assault on Cheatham's Hill (Mark A. Smith).

Introduction by Mark A. Smith

brigade to the south. By the next morning, Major Holmes described this Union position as "formidable."[45]

From this point until the early morning hours of July 3, the men of the two XIV Corps brigades remained in position, rejecting Davis's offer of relief and preferring instead to hold the ground that they had fortified themselves. They were not, however, inactive. The 125th Illinois, which had come up on the left of the 52nd Ohio on the afternoon of the twenty-seventh, advanced its lines about twenty feet the day after the assault through a tedious method developed by Lieutenant Colonel Langley and Corporal Joseph Frankenburg. These two men crawled forward under the cover of a tree in front of the regiment's position and dug a small pit; then they pulled empty cartridge and cracker boxes forward with a rope, filled them with dirt and placed them in front of their small pit as a parapet. This allowed more men to move forward and repeat the process, and the result was a line closer to the rebel defenses. Colonel Allen Fahnestock of the 86th Illinois on the right of the brigade advanced his line in a similar fashion on the night of June 28–29. In the center of the Third Brigade, though, the 52nd Ohio, the most advanced regiment at just thirty yards from the Confederate earthworks, merely held its position. Mitchell's men to the right of the Third Brigade also improved and advanced their works after dark on the twenty-eighth, and they tried to secure their right flank on the night of June 29–30. Their rebel opponents interpreted this move as a potential Federal attack and opened a firefight that halted work on Mitchell's right and more or less ended all attempts to move the Union lines forward in this sector. Lieutenant Colonel Langley, however, held a different view. He asserted in the official brigade report for the campaign that the brigade built a new line of works closer to Cheatham's Hill on June 30, a claim that Major Holmes flatly denied in his memoir, and one that historian Earl J. Hess also seems to reject when he asserts that Union men "never tried to dig closer to the enemy entrenchments than they were by June 29."[46]

Cheatham's southerners also took steps to improve their position and guard against a renewed Federal assault. The lines were too close to allow for the establishment of a picket line to provide warning in the event of an attack, so the rebels resorted to other means. After dark on June 28, they used ropes to lower a chevaux-de-frise over their parapet. Made of sharpened stakes attached to a central pole, a chevaux-de-frise provided an additional obstruction for any advancing Union soldiers. At the same time, Cheatham also ordered fireballs for his troops. These were cotton balls soaked in turpentine or tar; they were set afire and thrown into the no-man's-land between the two sets of trenches to provide illumination after dark and prevent a surprise night assault. When they were first used is uncertain, but the difficulty in procuring them suggests it was at least a few days after the June 27 attack; their employment may even have been responsible for the end of Federal attempts to move their positions forward after June 29.[47]

These improvements, both Union and Confederate, were necessary because musketry was nearly continuous along the lines at Cheatham's Hill, and on occasion, intense firefights developed as one side or the other reacted to a perceived threat. These usually happened at night, when the potential for a surprise assault was greater and the men were on edge, but vigilance was also required during daylight. Even though both sets of earthworks included head logs to protect the men on the firing line, anything appearing above the defenses drew fire, and men often fired at any shadows appearing between the head logs and the parapets. Major Holmes even reported the employment of what he called "billiard tactics" as some of his men fired at the bottom of the Confederate head logs trying, sometimes successfully, to ricochet their bullets down into the enemy's trenches. It is not surprising, then, that within a few days, this constant fire had eaten away much of the protection that the head logs provided. Even the Federal officers joined the sharpshooting across no-man's-land; at one point, Holmes borrowed a Henry repeating rifle from one of his men and focused so intently on using it that he inadvertently exposed himself. Other men in the Federal trenches displayed their Yankee ingenuity to protect themselves while maintaining fire. Someone in McCook's brigade, and it is not entirely clear who or even from which regiment, developed a refracting sight by attaching small mirrors to the stocks of their Enfield rifles. These allowed the men to rest the barrel of their guns on the parapet and, while they lay on their backs below the top of the trench, sight the rifle using the mirror and fire it without exposing themselves. This constant fire, however it was delivered, took its toll. Colonel Fahnestock reported an additional two men killed and eight wounded in

Introduction by Mark A. Smith

his 86th Illinois between June 27 and July 3 when the rebels evacuated, and the 52nd Ohio lost between twenty-three and thirty-four killed and wounded in this same period.[48]

The firing did slacken on occasion, and once it ceased entirely for nearly half a day. On the morning of June 29, the Johnnies and Yanks agreed to a grisly truce. Until that point, the bodies of the Federal soldiers killed in the June 27 assault beyond where McCook's and Mitchell's brigades later entrenched remained on the field. Given the heat of the early Georgia summer, the stench of putrefaction was soon overpowering. The truce was established to bury the dead, though officers and men from both sides came out of their lines and mingled in the no-man's-land while the burial details went about their gruesome task throughout most of the morning.[49]

The same day as the truce, McCook's brigade opened another avenue of approach to the rebel fortifications. That afternoon, Lieutenant Colonel Langley of the 125th Illinois opened a mine just behind the Union earthworks on the left flank of the 52nd Ohio about thirty-five yards from the Confederate breastworks. He hoped to reach the rebel line in time to pack the mine with gunpowder and detonate it on July 4. Progress was slow because he lacked specialized mining equipment and the men were unfamiliar with the work, but they took to it eagerly and nearly finished it. The mine was only about twenty-five feet short of its goal when Johnston evacuated his position at Kennesaw Mountain and retreated southward. Several members of the brigade erroneously attributed the rebel withdrawal to an alleged spy who, having seen the tunnel under construction, brazenly crossed from Union to Confederate lines in broad daylight on July 1 before any of the Federals could react quickly enough to stop him. The man, however, was neither a spy nor a deserter, but a confused soldier; Private Edward O'Donnell was still suffering the effects of sunstroke when he lost his way and crossed the no-man's-land to the rebel works. Only extraordinary luck let him make the trip without being killed. But in the long run his luck failed; taken prisoner, he died at Andersonville in September.[50]

A major point of contention about the Third Brigade's role at Cheatham Hill that emerged later was the relative positions of its regiments and the alleged practice of rotating them off the front line. This

Introduction by Mark A. Smith

issue, in part, motivated Holmes to prepare his twentieth-century memoir. Historian Earl J. Hess argues that from the afternoon of June 27—after the failure of the initial XIV Corps assault—through the withdrawal of Confederate forces in the early morning hours of July 3, the "commanders of both [McCook's and Mitchell's] brigades worked out a system of rotating the regiments in and out of the front line trenches." His main sources for this assertion of a regular system of regimental reliefs are: an 1896 account by Captain Frank James of the 52nd Ohio; the official campaign report of the Third Brigade by Lieutenant Colonel James W. Langley; the Second Division commander's campaign report; the reports of two regimental commanders from Mitchell's Second Brigade; a 1910 account by a former sergeant in the 34th Illinois of Mitchell's brigade; and two wartime diaries, one by Colonel Allen L. Fahnestock of the Third Brigade's 86th Illinois, and the other by an enlisted man from the 98th Ohio, Second Brigade.[51]

These alleged rotations in Mitchell's brigade can be dealt with relatively easily, particularly since Holmes did not belong to this unit and thus did not challenge these reliefs. The only two reports from the brigade or its constituent regiments that mention rotating units on and off the front lines are the two used by Hess, and they cite only two instances of regimental reliefs, involving only three of Mitchell's five regiments. The 34th Illinois reportedly relieved the 98th Ohio on the front line on June 30, and the 98th Ohio relieved the 78th Illinois after dark on July 2. A close examination of the 34th Illinois report, however, illustrates a *lack* of a system when it came to these rotations. Lieutenant Colonel Oscar Van Tassell recorded that on June 30, "I was ordered to relieve the Ninety-Eighth Ohio, then on the front line, *remaining under fire in the position left by them until the morning of July 3*" (emphasis added). Assuming that this exchange of regiments took place after dark on the thirtieth, when the movement had a better chance of occurring unnoticed by the enemy, then the 34th Illinois held a front-line position for about sixty hours, from the evening of June 30 through the morning of July 3 when the Confederates withdrew from the Kennesaw Line. Likewise, the 98th Ohio, on being relieved by Van Tassell's regiment on the evening of June 30, spent two days in the rear before relieving the 78th Illinois after dark on July 2. These two reliefs over a six-day period are also the *same* ones noted by Philip Ward, a diarist in the 98th Ohio, and the postwar accounts of Sergeants

Introduction by Mark A. Smith

Henry Pratt and Edwin Payne, both of the 34th Illinois. Payne even confirmed the timeline; he reported in 1903 that his regiment bivouacked about five hundred yards to the rear of the front line after the failed assault on June 27, and remained there until it relieved the 98th Ohio on the evening of the thirtieth, after which the Illinoisans spent "three days and two nights [on] ... the front line of rifle-pits." Given the lack of any other documented reliefs and the claims about the time spent on and off the front lines in these unofficial sources, the rotation of units in Mitchell's brigade seems to have been the exception rather than the rule. At the very least, they were hardly the "twenty-four hour shifts in the front line" that Hess describes.[52]

In McCook's brigade, the issue of these reliefs is murkier. The official report of the Third Brigade for the Atlanta Campaign was written by Lieutenant Colonel James W. Langley. He began June 27 serving on the XIV Corps staff of Major General John Palmer, but after Colonel Harmon of the 125th Illinois was killed while commanding the Third Brigade, Langley secured permission to return to and lead his regiment. He arrived in the late afternoon of the twenty-seventh and led the regiment from that time until Johnston's Confederates withdrew and Sherman's Federals pursued on July 3. He continued to command his regiment until September 1, when he took charge of the Third Brigade near the end of the Atlanta Campaign. As has been noted previously, Langley reported, perhaps inaccurately, that when he took charge of the 125th Illinois, the brigade was arranged with the 22nd Indiana on the front left, his own regiment in the front center, and the 85th Illinois on the front right, and according to him, at this point both the 52nd Ohio and the 86th Illinois were to the rear as the brigade's reserve. From these positions, Langley claimed in the brigade's official campaign report that the 86th Illinois relieved the 125th in the center of the brigade's front line position on the morning after the assault on Cheatham's Hill, and on the morning of the twenty-ninth, the 86th was itself relieved by the 52nd Ohio. Other than these two, Langley mentioned no other rotations of regiments in the Third Brigade.

There seems to be some confirmation of these events; Lieutenant Colonel Allen L. Fahnestock, commander of the 86th Illinois, reported the same two reliefs of regiments as well as two others in his wartime diary and in a postwar recollection based on that diary. On the morning of July 1, Fahnestock wrote that his regiment again relieved the 125th Illinois on the front line, though there is no evidence of when the 125th had *returned* to the front after allegedly being relieved on June 28. Fahnestock also reported that the 86th Illinois was again relieved by the 52nd Ohio during the morning of July 2, though when the 86th returned to the front after it had been relieved on June 29 is likewise undocumented. Interestingly, none of these sources mentions the relief of either the 22nd Indiana, which Langley claimed was on the brigade's left, or of the 85th Illinois on its right. Presumably, then, those two regiments held their positions throughout the five days following the assault without any relief, a situation that seems at odds with the claim of ongoing rotations in the center of the brigade's front line.[53]

There are also other evidentiary inconsistencies regarding these supposed regimental reliefs. Of the official reports from the Third Brigade's five constituent regiments, *none* describes any rotation of regiments on the front line. Four of those, however, were very brief reports of less than four printed pages; their authors may have believed these sorts of minor movements unworthy of notice in a report covering the entire Atlanta Campaign. The fifth one, though, was Fahnestock's report for the 86th Illinois, and while not substantially longer than the others, it does contain the illuminating remark that "My regiment, with the brigade, remained within twenty-five yards of the rebel works, keeping up an incessant fire until they fell back, on the night of July 2. During the six days we lay so close to the rebel works my regiment lost [an] additional 2 enlisted men killed and 8 wounded." This assertion that the 86th Illinois remained within twenty-five yards of the Confederate breastworks for six days implies that the regiment was *not* rotated off the front line, despite Fahnestock's claims in his diary. Likewise, James Holmes's wartime diary and correspondence, both of which he quoted from extensively in his 1898 memoir, imply that the 52nd Ohio remained on the front line of the Union position at Cheatham's Hill continuously from June 27 through July 3, without relief.[54]

Contradictory postwar accounts further confuse the issue. Leaving aside Fahnestock's postwar account based on his wartime diary, the 1896 recollections of Captain Frank James of the 52nd Ohio claim that the brigade's units rotated on and off the front line in twelve-hour shifts. No contemporary source supports a twelve-hour rotation, and while Holmes praised James's work in general in his 1898 memoir, he explicitly rejected this claim of twelve-hour reliefs in his later unpublished writings, adding that James "knew better." At the same time, according to Theodore Neighbor, the men of Company D, 52nd Ohio, spent "five days and nights" on the front line without so much as taking off their cartridge boxes, a specific memory at odds with the claims that Neighbor's regiment only rotated into the front lines for two days, June 29 and July 2. James Holmes, in the memoir that follows, specifically denied the claims that the 52nd Ohio moved off and on the front line in the days after the assault. He maintained with absolute certainty that his regiment stayed on the front line of the Third Brigade from June 27 through July 3, and because he himself had been stationed on the left of the 52nd Ohio, he was also fairly certain that the 125th Illinois was directly to its left for that entire period as well. Holmes's view is even confirmed by the tale of Lieutenant Colonel Langley and Corporal Frankenburg advancing the position of the 125th Illinois on the afternoon of June 28. According to Sergeant Robert M. Rogers of the 125th, Langley and Frankenburg achieved this feat using the cover provided by a large tree just in front of the regiment's position. This may have been the same large tree that Holmes mentioned as a landmark on the battlefield that was near the opening of the mine started on the twenty-ninth. If so, then the 125th Illinois would have been on the left of the brigade's front line, as Holmes claimed, and not in its center because by most accounts the tree and the mine were situated at the left of the brigade's center regiment and the right of its left-most regiment, where a unit's lieutenant colonel was typically stationed. Moreover, if the 125th was anywhere on the front line to advance the brigade's forward position on the afternoon of June 28, that flies in the face of claims by both Langley and Fahnestock that the regiment had been relieved of front-line duty on the morning of the twenty-eighth.[55]

While it is impossible to fully confirm Holmes's claim with the available evidence, there are other postwar accounts that support it. William Funston was a private in the 52nd Ohio, and he was detailed to hold the horse of its commander, Lieutenant Colonel Charles Clancy, during the June 27 assault. Clancy took a spent musket ball to his lower left leg early in the charge, before his men even reached the small creek at the bottom

Introduction by Mark A. Smith

of the valley between the Union and rebel positions. He hobbled along after his regiment, leaning on his sword and continuing in command, but later that day, long after the assault had failed, Clancy returned to the attack's launching point and met up with Funston who helped care for the officer's heavily bruised leg that night. As Funston remembered it thirty-five years later, Clancy *insisted* on visiting his regiment the next afternoon, the twenty-eighth, "and found it in the front line, and it was a hot place." This, then, was another specific postwar recollection at odds with the claims of Langley and Fahnestock, which both place the 52nd Ohio in reserve from the afternoon of June 27 until the morning of June 29. Moreover, Funston's tale lends credence to Holmes's claims in another way; when the lieutenant colonel left the field to tend to his bruised leg, he would have left the regiment under Major Holmes's command, at least until Clancy returned on the afternoon of the twenty-eighth, and Holmes's responsibilities in command of the 52nd Ohio would have provided him with clear knowledge of the unit's position. Similarly, a postwar map of the battlefield compiled by Julius Work in 1902 notes that the 125th Illinois, the 86th Illinois, and the 52nd Ohio built *and held* the Third Brigade's first line of works, implying that all three remained on the front line for some time.

This claim is further supported by the 1882 recollection of a member of the 125th Illinois who recalled his regiment serving "in the front line" throughout June 28, contradicting Langley's report that the regiment had been relieved that morning. Even the regimental casualty figures for the period from June 28 through the rebel withdrawal, as far as they can be ascertained, support Holmes's claim of an extended stay in an exposed position for the 52nd Ohio. Not all the units reported casualties for just this period, but official reports and postwar accounts provide numbers for two regiments, both of which were allegedly involved in the regimental rotations. Lieutenant Colonel Fahnestock reported ten additional casualties in the 86th Illinois during this period, two of which occurred on July 2 after Fahnestock alleged that the regiment had been relieved of front-line duty. According to Nixon Stewart, the 52nd Ohio lost thirty-four men killed and wounded in this period, while Holmes himself only remembered twenty-three additional casualties in his regiment along the Kennesaw Line. Even Holmes's lower number, though, was more than double the

Introduction by Mark A. Smith

losses of the Illinoisans, suggesting that Holmes's Buckeye regiment spent at least as much time, if not more than, exposed on the front line as the 86th Illinois. A precise regimental accounting may never be possible, but with the addition of the claims found in Holmes's memoir, it is at least clear that there was no regular system of regimental reliefs in McCook's Brigade in the days following the assault on Cheatham's Hill.[56]

Despite the controversy over these Union movements in front of the Dead Angle, the consequential position changes came elsewhere. By the early afternoon of June 27, it was clear to Sherman that he could not break Johnston's line near Kennesaw Mountain, and that same day Schofield's Federal Army of the Ohio had gained a position near the Confederate left that threatened the rebel line of retreat. Sherman wanted Schofield to press his advantage while McPherson's Army of the Tennessee moved from the Union left, behind Thomas in the center and past Schofield, to extend the Federal right and secure the railroad behind the rebel army. Before he could move off the railroad, though, McPherson needed to stockpile ten days' worth of supplies, which he had done by June 30. The next day, the Army of the Ohio started to push forward down the Sandtown Road on the Federal right. McPherson spent July 2 preparing for his flanking maneuver, and he put the Army of the Tennessee in motion about 9 o'clock that evening. Confederate cavalry scouts and rebels atop Kennesaw Mountain, however, reported McPherson's preparations to Johnston. The Confederate commander realized that his opponent was getting ready to turn the rebel left, and at 1:30 in the afternoon of July 2, he ordered a withdrawal that began at dusk.[57]

The men of McCook's brigade were some of the first Federals to learn of Johnston's withdrawal. About one o'clock on the morning of July 3, an unusual quiet descended on the lines along Cheatham's Hill, and several members of the brigade later remembered a lone rebel soldier asking them not to shoot him as he came over and surrendered. After he entered Union lines and reported the Confederate evacuation, Colonel Dilworth sent a small guard to verify his claim, and all these Federal soldiers found were empty trenches. The fighting around Kennesaw Mountain was over.[58]

The Atlanta Campaign, however, was not yet finished. Johnston's Confederates had only retreated three miles to a temporary position near

Introduction by Mark A. Smith

New Smyrna, which they held for two days until some light skirmishing convinced the rebel general to retreat to the north bank of the Chattahoochee River. The southern army remained north of the river until Sherman's men seized crossings on either flank of the Confederate position on July 8; on the ninth, Johnston retreated again to a point on the Marietta Road just three miles north of downtown Atlanta. While Federals paused just south of the Chattahoochee for a brief rest, Confederate President Jefferson Davis finally lost patience with Johnston's repeated withdrawals. On July 18, Davis replaced Johnson with the more aggressive John Bell Hood.[59]

Hood's appointment changed the nature of the campaign. In late July, he launched three attacks on Sherman's larger force and suffered three times as many casualties as he inflicted on the Federals. Thereafter, Hood concentrated on holding Atlanta while Sherman worked to cut all of the rail lines into the city to isolate Hood's army and force it to either surrender or to abandon Atlanta. Hood chose the latter option after he failed to prevent Union forces from cutting the railroad south of the city at the battle of the Jonesboro. The rebels evacuated on September 1, and the Atlanta Campaign ended the next day when Union forces occupied the city.[60]

While the fall of Atlanta ended the campaign and helped secure President Lincoln's re-election, guaranteeing that the war would continue until a complete Union victory, Atlanta's fall had *not* achieved Sherman's primary goal of destroying the Confederate Army of Tennessee. After abandoning the city, Hood took his army north and tried to sever the railroad supply line from Chattanooga. For much of September and October, Sherman's forces pursued him and defended the railroad while simultaneously occupying Atlanta. The Union commander eventually concluded that this sort of campaigning was a losing proposition and began to lay his own plans. He reorganized his forces and sent George Thomas north to Tennessee with about sixty thousand men; Thomas eventually achieved the utter ruin of Hood's army, but he did so without the XIV Corps that had been part of his army at Kennesaw. The sixty-seven thousand men that stayed with Sherman were divided into two wings, and the XIV Corps, including Dan McCook's old brigade and the 52nd Ohio with Major James Holmes, was in the left wing under Major General Henry Slocum's

Introduction by Mark A. Smith

command. Both wings of the newly-reorganized Federal force in Atlanta set out for Savannah in mid–November, beginning Sherman's famous marches.[61]

* * *

Long after it was over, the fighting at Kennesaw Mountain retained a special meaning for the men of the Third Brigade, Second Division, XIV Corps. They remembered the assault at Cheatham's Hill as some of the fiercest fighting that they faced in the war, and they lost a much-beloved commander when McCook fell. These events were so significant in their collective memory that it was the men of this brigade who began the memorialization of the battle. In the process, they made the first purchase of land that eventually led to the establishment of a national battlefield park to commemorate the fight along the Kennesaw Line.[62]

It began with postwar visits to the battlefield by survivors of the brigade, including one by Holmes. In 1897, he and his wife Lucy retraced the brigade's movements during the war, including the Atlanta Campaign, on a trip that was the basis for Holmes's 1898 printed memoir, *52d O.V.I.: Then and Now*. On this visit, he toured the battlefield at Cheatham's Hill and met the man who owned it, Virgil B. Channell. Holmes suggested preserving the area and its earthworks as a small park, but Channell thought it would be difficult to maintain as a private individual. Holmes later documented this much of his interactions with Channell in his 1898 reminiscences. In Chapter Two of this memoir, written in 1915, he asserted that after this visit he began corresponding with Channell about possibly buying a sixty-acre tract of land that included Cheatham's Hill and the Union and Confederate defensive works on and around it. According to Holmes, he and Channell had agreed on a sale for $1,350 when Channell changed his mind and Holmes let him out of the deal. Holmes only told one person about this agreement before it fell through, "a 52d officer of Cincinnati." He later suspected that this unnamed officer told three unidentified former members of the Third Brigade's Illinois regiments who, Holmes concluded, intentionally derailed his purchase so that they could buy the land instead. While historians of the battle and the park that was eventually established at its site acknowledge Holmes's 1897 visit, they have not reported on his attempt to buy the land. This would be a fruitful topic for further research,

The rear or western face of the Illinois monument, showing the text commemorating the actions of Illinois veterans above all others (Mark A. Smith).

given that Holmes claimed to have retained all of his correspondence with Channell on the subject as late as 1915.[63]

Circumstantial evidence suggests the plausibility of Holmes's claim. He believed the Illinois veterans who eventually bought the land around Cheatham's Hill were part of a clique that had been hostile to Colonel McCook during the war and who then sought to control the battleground to enhance the reputation of their state's contributions to the engagement. While this entire proposition is difficult to confirm, it *was* former members of the brigade's Illinois regiments who eventually played a leading role in the acquisition and memorialization of Cheatham's Hill. In 1896, a year *before* Holmes met Virgil Channell, the veterans of the 86th Illinois set up a committee at their regimental reunion to look into buying some land at Kennesaw Mountain to memorialize the fallen. This committee was also supposed to contact the other regimental organizations of the Third Brigade for their input. Nothing, however, was done until 1898 when the committee's chair approached Lansing J. Dawdy, a former sergeant in the 86th, and asked him to contact the other units. Dawdy found the idea popular with veterans from the other regiments, and in August 1899, the former members of the 86th Illinois authorized Dawdy to buy the land. In November, he visited Cheatham's Hill and struck a deal with Virgil Channell to buy sixty acres for a thousand dollars; the purchase was finalized on December 26, 1899.[64]

In February 1900, Dawdy transferred the land to two other veterans from the 86th Illinois, Martin Kingman and John McGinnis. These two men held the land in trust until a non-profit organization representing every unit from McCook's brigade was organized to administer the area and erect a monument to *all* the men of the brigade who had died at Cheatham's Hill. By the spring of 1901 the Kenesaw Memorial Association had been established under the laws of Illinois, and with the active support of all the brigade's units, it took over the sixty acres acquired at Cheatham's Hill along with the job of commemorating the men who fought and died there.[65]

The new non-profit immediately began efforts to raise money for a suitable monument. It began by contacting veterans of the brigade's regiments and soliciting contributions, but it quickly became apparent that the organization would never raise sufficient funds on its own. In 1907,

Introduction by Mark A. Smith

Photograph taken from the site of the rebel salient atop Cheatham's Hill, looking west over the deadly ground crossed by the men of the Third Brigade in their attack on the Confederate position (Mark A. Smith).

the group applied to the legislatures of Indiana, Ohio, and Illinois for financial support, and four years later Illinois lawmakers provided twenty thousand dollars to build a monument at Cheatham's Hill.[66]

While necessary to fund the monument, the involvement of the Illinois state legislature altered the project in a significant way, focusing it much more tightly on *Illinois* soldiers who fought at Cheatham's Hill rather than the entire Third Brigade. The 1911 law appropriating the money specified that "Whereas, [the] said Third Brigade [at Kennesaw Mountain] *was composed largely of Illinois troops, conspicuous for their courage and bravery*," the funding was provided "to be used for the erection of a monument on the battlefield of Kenesaw Mountain, Georgia, to the memory of the *Illinois soldiers* who died there on the 27th day of June, 1864" (emphasis

Introduction by Mark A. Smith

added). Moreover, the law authorized the state's governor to appoint three officers of the Kenesaw Memorial Association as commissioners to oversee the construction and placement of the monument at Cheatham's Hill. The association's officers had represented *all* of the units that composed McCook's brigade, but the new gubernatorial commissioners were all drawn from the Illinois units: Horace F. Reason, a former private in the 85th Illinois; Lansing J. Dawdy, formerly an 86th Illinois sergeant and the man who bought the land back in 1899; and William A. Payton, who had served as a musician in the 125th Illinois. Neither the 22nd Indiana nor the 52nd Ohio were represented on the new commission.[67]

Even the monument itself, its location, and its dedication ceremony all reinforced the new Illinois-centered direction of the commemoration project that had originally begun as a more inclusive operation aimed at all the men who had served under Colonel McCook at Kennesaw Mountain. The monument, designed by James Dibelka and sculpted out of Georgia marble by J. Mario Korbel, is a four-sided twenty-five-foot-tall structure. Its front side, facing the direction from which the Union assault came, contains a Union soldier flanked by two female figures, all beneath a banner framing a single word: "ILLINOIS." On the right face, the 85th and 86th Illinois's names and their June 27, 1864, commanders are carved into the marble; the left face lists the 125th Illinois and Battery I of the 2nd Illinois Light Artillery along with their commanders on the day of the assault, even though the battery served elsewhere on that summer morning in 1864. The rear of the monument contains a longer inscription:

> Erected to the memory
> of the
> ILLINOIS SOLDIERS
> who died on the battlefield of Kennesaw Mountain, Georgia June 27th, 1864.
> On this field the men of Col. Dan McCook's 3rd Brigade, 2nd Div., 14th Army Corps assaulted the Confederate works on the 27th day of June, 1864, losing four hundred and eighty killed and wounded, including two commanders, Col. Dan McCook mortally wounded and Col. O.F. Harmon killed; brigade reached Confederate works and at less than one hundred feet from them maintained a line for six days and nights without relief at the end of which time the Confederates evacuated.

Despite the inclusion of Battery I, which did not participate in the assault at Cheatham's Hill, no notice whatsoever was taken of the

Introduction by Mark A. Smith

22nd Indiana or the 52nd Ohio, even though the total number of casualties recorded on the monument represented the losses of the entire Third Brigade. This cenotaph, moreover, was located at the point in the Federal lines on Cheatham's Hill closest to the rebel entrenchments, a position, Holmes asserted in the memoir that follows, that was held by the 52nd Ohio throughout all Federal operations at Cheatham's Hill.[68]

The monument was dedicated June 27, 1914, the fiftieth anniversary of the assault, and the ceremony that day also highlighted the revised Illinois emphasis of the project. Illinois Governor Edward F. Dunne presided, and his remarks emphasized the contributions of soldiers from his own state. "We unveil this monument to the memory of those brave Illinoisians," Dunne announced," in a spirit of respect for the courage of the other brave men who gave up their lives on both sides, but in particular to commemorate ... the gallantry and heroism of Illinois troops." The monument had clearly become the *Illinois* monument, and *not* a commemoration of *all* of McCook's brigade. Indeed, the veterans of the 22nd Indiana and 52nd Ohio were lumped in with the Confederates by the governor's emphasis of the non–Illinois lives lost on "both sides."[69]

The Illinois focus of the new monument bothered the seventy-seven-year old James Holmes, who may have read some of Dunne's remarks in the newspapers. The dedication of the structure was what prompted him to produce Chapter Two of the new memoir presented here, which he finished in 1915, the year after the unveiling. He was not upset that Illinois was commemorating its native sons, but he was bothered by the fact that this monument solely to Illinoisans was situated on ground that, according to him, he and his Buckeye soldiers had taken and held throughout Union operations on Cheatham's Hill. And he had a point.[70] Long after the non-profit memorial organization transferred the Cheatham's Hill reservation to the United States and long after the federal government had expanded that small sixty-acre grant into the modern three-thousand acre Kennesaw Mountain National Battlefield Park, the structure atop Cheatham's Hill is still known as the *Illinois* monument, as Amanda Corman described it in her article for the sesquicentennial of the battle.[71] Holmes, however, would have had us acknowledge the contributions of the 52nd Ohio and also, I think it is safe to say, the 22nd Indiana. That is why he wrote this memoir,

Introduction by Mark A. Smith

to remedy for future generations the distortion that he believed this Illinois-centric commemoration had created.

NOTES

1. "James Taylor Holmes," in J. B. Work, ed., *Re-Union of Col. Dan McCook's Third Brigade, Second Division, Fourteenth A.C., Army of the Cumberland, August 27th and 29th, 1900* (Chicago: n.p., 1901), 86–87; Asa Holmes, 1850 U.S. Census, Harrison County, Ohio, population schedule, district 71, Short Creek Township, p. 462 (printed, 271 handwritten), dwelling 1875, family 1909, NARA microfilm publication M432, roll 692; Asa Holmes, 1860 U.S. Census, Harrison County, Ohio, population schedule, Short Creek Township, Short Creek Post Office, p. 52 (104 penned), dwelling 737, family 731, NARA microfilm publication M653, roll 984; Asa Holmes, 1870 U.S. Census, Harrison County, Ohio, population schedule, [Short Creek] Post Office, p. 10 (printed 206), dwelling 76, family 74, NARA microfilm publication M593, roll 1220.

2. "James Taylor Holmes," in Work, *Re-Union*, 87; John Wagoner, 1860 U.S. Census, Jefferson County, Ohio, population schedule, Salem Township, Richmond Post Office, p. 293 (133 penned), dwelling 961, family 952, NARA microfilm publication M653, roll 993.

3. "James Taylor Holmes," in Work, *Re-Union*, 87–88; J. T. Holmes, "The War Journal," in J. T. Holmes, *52d O.V.I.: Then and Now* (Columbus, OH: Berlin Printing Company, 1898), 1; *Official Roster of the Soldiers of the State of Ohio in the War of the Rebellion, 1861–1865* (Akron, OH: Werner Printing and Manufacturing Co., 1887), 4:663; Asa Holmes, 1850 U.S. Census, Harrison Co., OH, pop. sch., p. 462 (printed, 271 handwritten), dwell. 1875, fam. 1909; Whitelaw Reid, *Ohio in the War: Her Statesmen, Her Generals, and Soldiers*, 2 vols. (New York: Moore, Wilstach & Baldwin, 1868), 2:314; Leslie J. Perry, "Sketch of the Life of Brigadier-General Daniel McCook, Jr., U.S. Vols., Colonel 52d Ohio Vol. Infantry," in Work, *Re-Union*, 65, 71; J. T. Holmes to [his parents], 28 August 1862, in Holmes, *52d O.V.I.*, 50.

4. J. T. Holmes to [his parents], 28 August 1862, in Holmes, *52d O.V.I.*, 50; Nixon B. Stewart, *Dan. McCook's Regiment, 52nd O.V.I.: A History of the Regiment, Its Campaigns and Battles, from 1862 to 1865* (Alliance, OH: Review Print, 1900),12; Frederick H. Dyer, *A Compendium of the War of the Rebellion* (Des Moines, IA: Dyer Publishing, 1908), 1521; Kenneth W. Noe, *Perryville: This Grand Havoc of Battle* (Lexington: University Press of Kentucky, 2001), 39–40; Reid, *Ohio in the War*, 2:314–15; "James Taylor Holmes," in Work, *Re-Union*, 88; Holmes, *52d O.V.I.*, 69–79, 81–83; Holmes, "War Journal," 1–2.

5. Stewart, *Dan. McCook's Regiment*, 20, 22–23; Perry, "Life of McCook," in Work, *Re-Union*, 73; Reid, *Ohio in the War*, 2:315; Dyer, *Compendium*, 1521; Noe, *Perryville*, 148; "Organization of Col. Dan McCook's Brigade," in Work, *Re-Union*, 98.

6. Holmes, *52d O.V.I.*, 90–95; Holmes, "War Journal," 2–3; Dyer, *Compendium*, 1521; Perry, "Life of McCook," in Work, *Re-Union*, 73; Reid, *Ohio in the War*, 2:315; Stewart, *Dan. McCook's Regiment*, 25–28, 32–36, 38; "Organization of Col. Dan McCook's Brigade," in Work, *Re-Union*, 98.

7. Holmes, "War Journal," 3–4; Reid, *Ohio in the War*, 2:316; Stewart, *Dan. McCook's Regiment*, 47–49, 207; Holmes, *52d O.V.I.*, 112–13, 115; Dyer, *Compendium*, 1521.

8. Dyer, *Compendium*, 1521; Holmes, *52d O.V.I.*, 117, 133; Holmes, "War Journal," 4–6; J. T. Holmes to his sister, 18 September 1863, in Holmes, *52d O.V.I.*, 120–23; Stewart, *Dan. McCook's Regiment*, 52–55; J. T. Holmes to Sue, 29 September 1863, in Holmes, *52d O.V.I.*, 123–24; Reid, *Ohio in the War*, 2:316–17; "Organization of Col. Dan McCook's Brigade," in Work, *Re-Union*, 98.

9. Holmes to Anderson, 10 October 1863, in United States War Department, *The War of the Rebellion: A Compilation of the Official Records of the Union and Confederate Armies*,

Introduction by Mark A. Smith

4 series, 128 vols. (Washington, DC: Government Printing Office, 1880–1901), ser. 1, 30(i):879–882 (cited hereafter as *OR*, volume(part, if used):page, with all citations to series 1); Peter Cozzens, *This Terrible Sound: The Battle of Chickamauga* (Chicago: University of Illinois Press, 1992), 121–24; William M. Lamers, *The Edge of Glory: A Biography of General William S. Rosecrans, U.S.A.*, intro. Larry J. Daniels (Baton Rouge: Louisiana State University Press, 1999), 327; J. T. Holmes to Sue, 30 September 1863, in Holmes, *52d O.V.I.*, 125; Holmes, *52d O.V.I.*, 134.

10. Holmes, "War Journal," 6; Cozzens, *This Terrible Sound*, 440–42, 494, 510; J. T. Holmes to Sue, 30 September 1863, in Holmes, *52d O.V.I.*, 25–27; Holmes, *52d O.V.I.*, 139–140; Reid, *Ohio in the War*, 2:317.

11. Reid, *Ohio in the War*, 2:317–18; Lamers, *Edge of Glory*, 391–92; 399–400; "Organization of Col. Dan McCook's Brigade," in Work, *Re-Union*, 98; Dyer, *Compendium*, 1521; Holmes, *52d O.V.I.*, 107, 153; John Bowers, *Chickamauga and Chattanooga: The Battles that Doomed the Confederacy* (New York: HarperCollins, 1994), 189–195.

12. Holmes, "War Journal," 8; Stewart, *Dan. McCook's Regiment*, 70–71; Holmes to Anderson, 19 December 1863, in *OR*, 31(ii):505–506; Reid, *Ohio in the War*, 2:318.

13. Sherman to Rawlins, 19 December 1863, in *OR*, 31(ii):578; Thomas to Thomas, 1 December 1863, in *OR*, 31(ii):97; Stewart, *Dan. McCook's Regiment*, 23, 77, 79, 81, 84–86; Dyer, *Compendium*, 35; Holmes, *52d O.V.I.*, 150, 157, 160; Holmes, "War Journal," 8–9; Reid, *Ohio in the War*, 2:318–19.

14. J. T. Holmes to his parents, 14 September 1864, in Holmes, *52d O.V.I.*, 256; "James Taylor Holmes," in Work, *Re-Union*, 96; Holmes, "War Journal," 15; Holmes, *52d O.V.I.*, 216–17.

15. Holmes, *52d O.V.I.*, 266, 269–270; Davis to McClurg, — September 1864, in *OR*, 38(i):516; Sherman to Grant, 28 September 1864, in *OR*, 39(ii):502; Sherman to Halleck, 29 September 1864, in *OR*, 39(ii):517; J. T. Holmes to Sister Em, 26 October 1864, in Holmes, *52d O.V.I.*, 260–61; Stewart, *Dan. McCook's Regiment*, 139–141; Holmes, "War Journal," 16–17.

16. Holmes, "War Journal," 16–19, 25, 28–29, 31, 33, 36–38; Stewart, *Dan. McCook's Regiment*, 152, 159–162, 170–71, 173–74, 176–77, 179–180, 182; Reid, *Ohio in the War*, 2:319; Mark L. Bradley, *This Astounding Close: The Road to Bennett Place* (Chapel Hill: University of North Carolina Press, 2000), 20–24.

17. "James Taylor Holmes," in Work, *Re-Union*, 88–89; *Dayton (Ohio) Journal*, 31 December [1895], in Work, *Re-Union*, 97.

18. "James Taylor Holmes," in Work, *Re-Union*, 89; Herman Alfred Kelley, comp., *A Genealogical History of the Kelley Family Descended from Joseph Kelley of Norwich, Connecticut* (Cleveland, OH: 1897), 101–102; J. T. Holmes, 1880 U.S. Census, Franklin County, Ohio, population schedule, Columbus, enumeration district (ED) 27, p. 163 (stamped), p. 2 (penned), dwelling 12, family 13, NARA microfilm publication T9, roll 1016; James Holmes, 1900 U.S. Census, Franklin County, Ohio, population schedule, City of Columbus, ward 11, sheet 23 (handwritten, 204A printed), enumeration district (ED) 93, dwelling 185, family 205; NARA microfilm publication T623, roll 1269; James T. Holmes, 1910 U.S. Census, Franklin County, Ohio, population schedule, City of Columbus, ward 6, enumeration district (ED) 102, sheet 2a (handwritten), dwelling 34, family 35, NARA microfilm publication T624, roll 1181; Certificate of Death of James Taylor Holmes, in Widow's Pension Application, Claim No. 1065297, Certificate No. 813006, James T. Holmes (Co. G, 52nd Ohio Infantry), Civil War and Later Pension Files, Record Group 15, Records of the Department of Veterans Affairs, National Archives and Records Administration, Washington, DC.

19. Earl J. Hess, *Kennesaw Mountain: Sherman, Johnston, and the Atlanta Campaign* (Chapel Hill: University of North Carolina Press, 2013), 1; Sherman to Halleck, 8 June 1864 in *OR*, 38(i):617; Sherman to Halleck, 15 September, in *OR*, 38(i):62–63; Grant to Sherman,

Introduction by Mark A. Smith

4 April 1864, in William Tecumseh Sherman, *Memoirs of General W. T. Sherman*, Library of America series No. 51, edited by Charles Royster (Boone, IA: Library of America, 1990), 490. Much of the following discussion of the Atlanta Campaign and the battle of Kennesaw Mountain depends on the two most comprehensive secondary accounts of those operations: Hess's *Kennesaw Mountain* (cited in full above) and Albert Castel's *Decision in the West: The Atlanta Campaign of 1864* (Lawrence: University Press of Kansas, 1992).

20. Hess, *Kennesaw Mountain*, 1–2; Castel, *Decision in the West*, 69, 106–112; Sherman to Halleck, 8 June 1864, in *OR*, 38(i):61; Sherman to Halleck, 15 September 1864, in *OR*, 38(i):62; William T. Sherman, "The Grand Strategy of the Last Year of the War," in *Battles and Leaders of the Civil War*, 4 vols., ed. Robert Underwood Johnston and Clarence Clough Buel (New York: Century Company, 1887–1888), 4:250–52; John F. Marszalek, *Sherman: A Soldier's Passion for Order* (New York: Free Press, 1993), 261, 264.

21. Sherman to Halleck, 15 September 1864, in *OR*, 38(i):63–64; Castel, *Decision in the West*, 121–23, 138–39, 144–150; Hess, *Kennesaw Mountain*, 2–3; James M. McPherson, *Battle Cry of Freedom: The Civil War Era*, Oxford History of the United States series (Oxford: Oxford University Press, 1988), 744–75.

22. Sherman to Halleck, 15 September 1864, in *OR*, 38(i):64–65; Castel, *Decision in the West*, 151–53, 159–179; Hess, *Kennesaw Mountain*, 3.

23. Castel, *Decision in the West*, 191–95, 199–205; Sherman to Halleck, 15 September 1864, in *OR*, 38(i): 65; Hess, *Kennesaw Mountain*, 3.

24. Sherman, *Memoirs*, 511–12; Hess, *Kennesaw Mountain*, 5; Castel, *Decision in the West*, 213–14, 218–19; Sherman to Halleck, 15 September 1864, in *OR*, 38(i): 65.

25. Sherman to Halleck, 15 September 1864, in *OR*, 38(i):65–67; Sherman, *Memoirs*, 512–15, 519; Castel, *Decision in the West*, 209–217-226, 228–252, 256–261; Hess, *Kennesaw Mountain*, 5.

26. Sherman to Halleck, 15 September 1864, in *OR*, 38(i):67; Sherman, *Memoirs*, 520–26; Castel, *Decision in the West*, 267–69, 275–76, 279–284; Hess, *Kennesaw Mountain*, 6–15; Craig L. Symonds, *Joseph E. Johnston: A Civil War Biography* (New York: W. W. Norton, 1992), 307; Joseph E. Johnston, *Narrative of Military Operations during the Civil War*, intro. Frank E. Vandiver (Bloomington: Indiana University Press, 1959), 338; Holmes to Swift, 7 September 1864, in *OR*, 38(i):729.

27. Hess, *Kennesaw Mountain*, 15–18, 51; Sherman to Halleck, 15 September 1864, in *OR*, 38(i):67–68; Castel, *Decision in the West*, 285, 290; Symonds, *Johnston*, 312.

28. Sherman to Halleck, 15 September 1864, in *OR*, 38(i):68; Hess, *Kennesaw Mountain*, 18–40; Sherman, *Memoirs*, 527–28; Castel, *Decision in the West*, 288–295; Symonds, *Johnston*, 309.

29. Sherman, *Memoirs*, 530–31; Hess, *Kennesaw Mountain*, 49–51, 62–63; Castel, *Decision in the West*, 299–301; Sherman to Halleck, 15 September 1864, in *OR*, 38(i):68; Special Field Orders No. 28, Military Division of the Mississippi, 24 June 1864, in *OR*, 38(iv):588.

30. Special Field Orders No. 28, Military Division of the Mississippi, 24 June 1864, in *OR*, 38(iv):588; Sherman to Halleck, 15 September 1864, in *OR*, 38(i):68–69; Howard to Whipple, 18 September 1864, in *OR*, 38(i):199; Davis to McClurg, — September 1864, in *OR*, 38(i):632; Hess, *Kennesaw Mountain*, 57, 63–64, 66, 71–85; Castel, *Decision in the West*, 303–305.

31. Hess, Kennesaw Mountain, 57; Castel, Decision in the West, 313.

32. Ibid; Samuel Robinson, "Battle of Kennesaw Mountain: Part Borne by the First and Twenty-Seventh (Consolidated) Tennessee Regiments, Maney's Brigade," in *The Annals of the Army of Tennessee and Early Western History*, ed. Edwin L. Drake (Nashville, TN: A. D. Haynes, 1878), 109–110; [T. H. Maney], "The Battle of the Dead Angle on the Kennesaw Line, Near Marietta, Georgia," *Southern Bivouac* 3, no. 2 (October 1884), 72; Symonds, *Johnston*, 314.

Introduction by Mark A. Smith

33. Hess, *Kennesaw Mountain*, 57–59; Christopher Losson, *Tennessee's Forgotten Warriors: Frank Cheatham and His Confederate Division* (Knoxville: University of Tennessee Press, 1989), 153–54; quote from Castel, *Decision in the West*, 313; Maney, "The Dead Angle," 71; Robinson, "Battle of Kennesaw Mountain," 110; Charles Royster, *The Destructive War: William Tecumseh Sherman, Stonewall Jackson, and the Americans* (New York: Random House, 1991), 313.

34. Hess, *Kennesaw Mountain*, 57–62; Robinson, "Battle of Kennesaw Mountain," 110; Castel, *Decision in the West*, 313; Davis to McClurg, — September 1864, in *OR*, 38(i):632; Royster, *Destructive War*, 304, 313; Sam Watkins, *"Company Aytch" or, A Side Show of the Big Show*, ed. M. Thomas Inge (New York: Plume, 1999), 130, 236; Losson, *Tennessee's Forgotten Warriors*, 153–54.

35. Hess, *Kennesaw Mountain*, 68–69, 96; Castel, *Decision in the West*, 304–305; "Itinerary of the Fourteenth Army Corps, May 6 – September 8 [1864]," in *OR*, 38(i):506; Special Field Orders No. —, Department of the Cumberland, 26 June 1864, in *OR*, 39(iv):602; Morgan to Morrison, 23 August 1864, in *OR*, 38(i):680; Fahnestock to Swift, 7 September 1864, in *OR*, 38(i):721; Snodgrass to Swift, 7 September 1864, in *OR*, 38(i):726.

36. Banning to Wilson 9 September 1864, in *OR*, 38(i):703; Henry J. Aten, *History of the Eighty-Fifth Regiment, Illinois Volunteer Infantry* (Hiawatha, KS: n.p., 1901), 181–82; Holmes to Swift, 7 September 1864, in *OR*, 38(i):729; Mitchell to Wiseman, 4 September 1864, in *OR*, 38(i):680; Holmes, *52d O.V.I.*, 178; Castel, *Decision in the West*, 309; Langley to Wiseman, 9 September 1864, in *OR*, 38(i):710; F. B. James, "McCook's Brigade at the Assault Upon Kenesaw Mountain, Georgia, June 27, 1864," in W. H. Chamberlin, ed., *Sketches of War History* (Cincinnati, OH: Robert Clarke Company, 1896), 256–57; Earl J. Hess, *Civil War Infantry Tactics: Training, Combat, and Small-Unit Effectiveness* (Baton Rouge: Louisiana State University Press, 2015), 49–51, 141, 150, 244, 247.

37. Howard to Whipple, 18 September 1864, in *OR*, 38(i):199 (quoted); Newton to Assistant Adjutant-General, Headquarters Army of the Cumberland, — September 1864, in *OR*, 38(i):295; Castel, *Decision in the West*, 307, 316–17; James, "McCook's Brigade," 256–57; Hess, *Kennesaw Mountain*, 96–97, 113–14; Hess, *Civil War Infantry Tactics*, 51, 141, 158, 244; Royster, *Destructive War*, 310–12. It should be noted that Earl J. Hess argues that Wagner and Kimball attacked in a more traditional column of regiments like McCook and Mitchell. However, Howard, as quoted in the main text, clearly indicated that both his columns had the front of a regimental division, suggesting that they both used the same assault formation. Either way, however, the gaps between Howard's columns and the relatively narrow fronts of the columns themselves undermined the efficacy of his attack. See also Hess, *Kennesaw Mountain*, 97, and Hess, *Civil War Infantry Tactics*, 158.

38. Royster, *Destructive War*, 306–307, 312–13; Langley to Wiseman, 9 September 1864, in *OR*, 38(i):710; Davis to McClurg, — September 1864, in *OR*, 38(i):632; James, "McCook's Brigade," 258–59; W. J. Funston Recollection in Work, *Re-Union*, 30; Hess, *Kennesaw Mountain*, 114, 116–18, 283n13; Aten, *Eighty-Fifth Illinois*, 181–82, 185; Jonathon Moore, "Kenesaw Mountain: The Conduct of the Fourth and Fourteenth Corps at the Charge," *Washington National Tribune*, 3 April 1890.

39. Hess, *Kennesaw Mountain*, 117–21; Aten, *Eighty-Fifth Illinois*, 181–82, 185; Langley to Wiseman, 9 September 1864, in *OR*, 38(i):710; James, "McCook's Brigade," 258–59; Royster, *Destructive War*, 313; L. J. Dawdy Recollection in Work, *Re-Union*, 35.

40. Hess, *Kennesaw Mountain*, 119–124; Hess, *Eighty-Fifth Illinois*, 185; James, "McCook's Brigade," 259–260; Samuel Grimshaw Recollection, in Work, *Re-Union*, 43; Royster, *Destructive War*, 313–14; "History of the One Hundred and Twenty-Fifty [Illinois] Infantry," in Work, *Re-Union*, 128; Stewart, *Dan. McCook's Regiment*, 118–19; Langley to Wiseman, 9 September 1864, in *OR*, 38(i):711; Holmes, *52d O.V.I.*, 180–83; Castel, *Decision in the West*, 314; J. T. Holmes, "Assault on Kenesaw Mountain, Ga., June 27th, 1864, by Col. Dan.

Introduction by Mark A. Smith

McCook's Brigade," in Work, *Re-Union*, 78; Holmes to Swift, 7 September 1864, in *OR*, 38(i):729; Sam M. Pyle Recollection, in Work, *Re-Union*, 62.

41. Royster, *Destructive War*, 314–15; Holmes, *52d O.V.I.*, 185; Aten, *Eighty-Fifty Illinois*, 186–87; Pyle Recollection, in Work, *Re-Union*, 62; Hess, *Kennesaw Mountain*, 125–27, 149; Samuel Grimshaw Recollection, in Work, *Re-Union*, 43; James, "McCook's Brigade," 261–62; Castel, *Decision in the West*, 314–15; Stewart, *Dan. McCook's Regiment*, 119–120; Holmes to Swift, 7 September 1864, in *OR*, 38(i):729; I. M. Gray, "Kenesaw: What the Third Brigade, Second Division, Fourteenth Corps, Did on the Eventful June 27," *Washington National Tribune*, 15 November 1894; Moore, "Kenesaw Mountain"; E. M. Payne, "At Kenesaw: A 34th Ill. Man Tells What He Saw There," *Washington National Tribune*, 25 May 1893; Dawdy Recollection, in Work, *Re-Union*, 35; Langley to Wiseman, 9 September 1864, in *OR*, 38(i):711; Sherman, *Memoirs*, 531.

42. Hess, *Kennesaw Mountain*, 149; Langley to Wiseman, 9 September 1864, in *OR*, 38(i):711, 714; J. T. Holmes, "Movements and Positions in the Kenesaw Battle, June 27th – July 2nd, 1864," (typescript, private collection of Garth Bishop, Hopewell Junction, New York), 3, 11–16, 22–23, 30–37.

43. Hess, Kennesaw Mountain, 128–130; Castel, Decision in the West, 314.

44. Hess, *Kennesaw Mountain*, 127, 144–45, 153; Sherman, *Memoirs*, 531; Castel, *Decision in the West*, 314–15; Royster, *Destructive War*, 315–16; Davis to McClurg, 28 June 1864, in *OR*, 38(i):637; J. T. Holmes, "List of Casualties in the Fifty-second Ohio Infantry Volunteers from May 8, 1864, to September 5, 1864," in *OR*, 38(i):731.

45. Hess, *Kennesaw Mountain*, 148–49, 151–52; James, "McCook's Brigade," 261; Royster, *Destructive War*, 316–17; Stewart, *Dan. McCook's Regiment*, 124; Aten, *Eighty-Fifth Illinois*, 186–87; Holmes, *52d O.V.I.*, 185.

46. Royster, *Destructive War*, 317; Hess, *Kennesaw Mountain*, 165–66, 171–74, quote from 173; Robert M. Rogers, *The 125th Regiment Illinois Volunteer Infantry* (Champion, IL: Gazette Steam Print, 1882), 98; Allen L. Fahnestock to J. B. Work, 1901, in Work, *Re-Union*, 38; Holmes, *52d O.V.I.*, 191; Langley to Wiseman, 9 September 1864, in *OR*, 38(i):711; Holmes, "Movements and Positions," 34. There are several postwar accounts that seem to support Langley's assertion of a new, more advanced brigade line being constructed on June 30, but these may in fact be *based* on Langley's report. See also page 264 of James, "McCook's Brigade," which appeared in 1890, five years after the volume of the *OR* containing Langley's report was published, and pages 189 and 190 of Aten's *Eighty-Fifth Illinois*, which appeared five years after James's article.

47. Hess, *Kennesaw Mountain*, 166, 181; John L. Shellenberger, "Kenesaw Mountain: The Causes That Led to the Repulse of Harker's Brigade," *Washington National Tribune*, 11 December 1890; Watkins, *"Company Aytch,"* 134, 239–240; Holmes, *52d O.V.I.*, 197; Royster, *Destructive War*, 317; Castel, *Decision in the West*, 324; James, "McCook's Brigade," 263; Benning to Wilson, 9 September 1864, in *OR*, 38(i):704; Stewart, *Dan. McCook's Regiment*, 124, 126; Aten, *Eighty-Fifth Illinois*, 189–190; Allen L. Fahnestock to J. B. Work, 1901, in Work, *Re-Union*, 39; I. M. Gary, "Kenesaw: What the Third Brigade, Second Division, Fourteenth Corps, Did on the Eventful June 27," *Washington National Tribune*, 1894.

48. T. D. Neighbor, "Kenesaw Mountain: The Part Taken by McCook's Brigade in the Charge," *Washington National Tribune*, 25 December 1890; Stewart, *Dan. McCook's Regiment*, 126–28; Banning to Wilson, 9 September 1864, in *OR*, 38(i):704; James, "McCook's Brigade," 265, Hess, *Kennesaw Mountain*, 171–73, 177–79, 181–82; Edwin M. Payne, *History of the Thirty-Fourth Regiment of Illinois Volunteer Infantry, September 7, 1861 – July 12, 1865* (Clinton, IA: Allen Printing, 1903), 133; Holmes, *52d O.V.I.*, 185–85; Castel, *Decision in the West*, 324; J. B. Work, "Gun Glasses," in Work, *Re-Union*, 121; Samuel Grimshaw Recollection, in Work, *Re-Union*, 43; Allen Fahnestock to J. B. Work, 1901, in Work, *Re-Union*, 38; Langley to Wiseman, 9 September 1864, in *OR*, 38(i):711; Watkins, *"Company Aytch,"*

Introduction by Mark A. Smith

136; Fahnestock to Swift, 7 September 1864, in *OR*, 38(i):721. After the war, J. B. Work of the 52nd Ohio identified Lieutenant E. C. Silliman of the 86th Illinois as the inventor of the refracting sight, but Work was not serving with the regiment at the time of the battle at Kennesaw Mountain. Nixon Stewart, also from the Ohio regiment, claimed that an unnamed enlisted man from the 125th Illinois had developed the ingenious device. See also J. B. Work, "Gun Glasses," in Work, *Re-Union*, 121, and Stewart, *Dan. McCook's Regiment*, 127.

49. Holmes, *52d O.V.I.*, 187–88; Hess, *Kennesaw Mountain*, 166–67; Royster, *Destructive War*, 318; Aten, *Eighty-Fifth Illinois*, 187; James, "McCook's Brigade," 263; Johnston, *Narrative*, 344; Castel, *Decision in the West*, 323–24.

50. Allen L. Fahnestock to J. B. Work, 1901, in Work, *Re-Union*, 38–39; Holmes, *52d O.V.I.*, 187; Hess, *Kennesaw Mountain*, 177, 182–183; Rogers, *125th Illinois*, 98; Aten, *Eighty-Fifth Illinois*, 190; Castel, *Decision in the West*, 324; James, "McCook's Brigade," 264–65; John Moore, "A Rebel Spy," *Washington National Tribune*, 4 November 1895; Stewart, *Dan. McCook's Regiment*, 127–28; Payne, *Thirty-Fourth Illinois*, 134–35. In the memoir that follows, Holmes argued that the 52nd Ohio built this mine, though he was not nearly so strident on this issue as he was about the regimental positions and their reliefs discussed below in the main text of the introduction.

51. Hess, *Kennesaw Mountain*, 165, 174–75, quote from 165. The materials that Hess cites in support of this system of reliefs within the two brigades are: James, "McCook's Brigade," 262; Langley to Wiseman, 9 September 1864, in *OR*, 38(i):711; Davis to McClurg, — September 1864, in *OR*, 38(i):633; Van Tassell to Wilson, 5 September 1864, in *OR*, 38(i):686; Pearce to Wilson, 9 September 1864, in *OR*, 38(i):693; Allen L. Fahnestock Diary, June 28–29, July 1–2, 1864, Allen L. Fahnestock Papers, 1863–1865 & 1902 (Manuscript SC 472), Abraham Lincoln Presidential Library, Springfield, IL; and Philip R. Ward Diary, June 30, July 1–2, 1864 in Charles S. Harris Collection, Special Collections, University of Tennessee at Chattanooga. See also Hess, *Kennesaw Mountain*, 291–92n2, 294n36.

52. Mitchell to Wiseman, 4 September 1864, in *OR*, 38(i):680; Vernon to Wiseman, 5 September 1864, in *OR*, 38(i):688: Jones to Wilson, 10 September 1864, in *OR*, 38(i):698; Banning to Wilson, 9 September 1864, in *OR*, 38(i):704, quote from Van Tassell to Wilson, 5 September 1864, in *OR*, 38(i):686; Pearce to Wilson 9 September 1864, in *OR*, 38(i):693; quote from Hess, *Kennesaw Mountain*, 175; Henry C. Pratt, "After the Assault at Kenesaw," *Washington National Tribune*, 28 July 1910; Ward Diary, June 30, July 1–2, 1864; Payne, *Thirty-Fourth Illinois*, 129, 133, 135, quote from 135.

53. Langley to Wiseman, 9 September 1864, in *OR*, 38(i):711; Fahnestock Diary, June 28–29, July 1–2, 1864; Allen L. Fahnestock to J. B. Work, 1901, in Work, *Re-Union*, 38–39. It is also possible that Langley's official brigade report and its mention of two regimental rotations was based in part on Fahnestock's diary. Langley noted that for his report on operations from June 27 through early September, he was "chiefly reliant for information on the notes and memoranda of Colonel Dilworth, commanding the brigade." This leaves open the possibility that he also consulted *other* sources like Fahnestock's diary, which could explain the similar claims made by these two contemporary sources in light of the evidentiary inconsistencies examined in the next paragraph of the main introductory text.

54. Snodgrass to Swift, 7 September 1864, in *OR*, 38(i):726; Holmes to Swift, 7 September 1864, in *OR*, 38(i):729; Griffith to Swift, 7 September 1864, in *OR*, 38(i):718; Cook to Swift, 7 September 1864, in *OR*, 38(i):724; quote from Fahnestock to Swift, 7 September 1864, in *OR*, 38(i):721; J. T. Holmes, "War Journal," in Holmes, *52d O.V.I.*, 12; J. T. Holmes to his parents, 19 July 1864, in Holmes, *52d O.V.I.*, 236; J. T. Holmes to his father, [1864], in Holmes, *52d O.V.I.*, 183.

55. James, "McCook's Brigade," 262, 265; Holmes, *52d O.V.I.*, 180; T. D. Neighbor, "Kenesaw Mountain: The Part Taken by McCook's Brigade in the Charge," *Washington National*

Introduction by Mark A. Smith

Tribune, 25 December 1890; Holmes, "Movements and Positions," 2–3, 12, 14, 33–34, 110; Rogers, *125th Illinois*, 98; Fahnestock Diary, 28 June 1864, Langley to Wiseman, 9 September 1864, in *OR*, 38(i):711.

56. Funston Recollection, in Work, *Re-Union*, 30; J. B. Work, "Map of the 'Dead Angle,' Cheatham's Hill, Kenesaw Mountain, Ga., June 27 – July 2–3, 1864," 1902, in *Confederate Veteran* Papers, David M. Rubenstein Rare Book & Manuscripts Library, Duke University, Durham, NC; Rogers, *125th Illinois*, 98; Hess, *Kennesaw Mountain*, 118–119, 178; Fahnestock to Swift, 7 September 1864, in *OR*, 38(i):721; Fahnestock Diary, June 28–29, July 1–2, 1864, and p. 250 (undated); Allen L. Fahnestock to J. B. Work, 1901, in Work, *Re-Union*, 38–39; Stewart, *Dan. McCook's Regiment*, 128. It also worth noting that Holmes, in his early-twentieth century memoir that makes up the bulk of this volume, went so far as to accuse Fahnestock (though not by name) of fabricating his wartime diary and his tale of regimental reliefs years after the war as part of a plot to enhance the reputation of the Illinois regiments in the brigade, at the expense of the 52nd Ohio. See also chapter two of this published memoir and related annotations.

57. Castel, *Decision in the West*, 317, 322, 324–25; Sherman, *Memoirs*, 531–32; Sherman to Halleck, 15 September 1864, in *OR*, 38(i):69; Thomas to Sawyer, 17 August 1864, in *OR*, 38(i):154; Hess, *Kennesaw Mountain*, 176, 188–190, 193, 195–97; Royster, *Destructive War*, 318; Johnston, *Narrative*, 345; Payne, *Thirty-Fourth Illinois*, 135.

58. Hess, *Kennesaw Mountain*, 199–200; James, "McCook's Brigade," 265–66; Stewart, *Dan. McCook's Regiment*, 129; Castel, *Decision in the West*, 329–330; Allen L. Fahnestock to J. B. Work, 1901, in Work, *Re-Union*, 39.

59. Hess, *Kennesaw Mountain*, 199, 210–211, 213; Symonds, *Johnston*, 316–17; Castel, *Decision in the West*, 336, 339, 341, 361.

60. See Castel, *Decision in the West*, 368–529, for a detailed recounting of these events.

61. Lee Kennett, *Marching through Georgia: The Story of Soldiers & Civilians during Sherman's Campaign* (New York: HarperCollins, 1995), 217–229; Marszalek, *Sherman*, 288–295; "The Savannah (Georgia) Campaign. No. 2—Organization of the Union forces, commanded by Maj. Gen. William T. Sherman," in *OR*, 44:22–23.

62. Sam M. Pyle Recollection, in Work, *Re-Union*, 61; "James Taylor Holmes," in Work, *Re-Union*, 86.

63. Holmes, *52d O.V.I.*, 41–42, 190, Holmes, "Movements and Positions," 56–59, 61, quote from 58; Hess, *Kennesaw Mountain*, 236–37; Amanda Corman, "Kennesaw Mountain's Illinois Monument: Commemorating the Past, Honoring the Present, Inspiring the Future," *The Sentinel*, Special Edition: 150th Anniversary of the Atlanta Campaign (2014): 27; Michael A. Capps, *Kennesaw Mountain National Battlefield Park: Administrative History* (Atlanta, GA: Southeast Regional Office, National Park Service, Department of the Interior, 1994), chapter 2, online source, accessed 8 October 2017, https://www.nps.gov/parkhistory/online_books/kemo/adhi/adhi.html. The Cincinnati officer from the 52nd Ohio that Holmes mentioned may have been former Captain Frank B. James of that city, but this is not entirely certain. For James's postwar city of residence, see "Kennesaw Memorial Association Perfects Its Organization," *Indianapolis Journal*, 11 August 1901.

64. Holmes, "Movements and Positions," 47, 58–59; "L. J. Dawdy Report," in Work, *Re-Union*, 10–11; Corman, "Illinois Monument," 27; Capps, *Administrative History*, ch. 2; Hess, *Kennesaw Mountain*, 237.

65. Hess, *Kennesaw Mountain*, 237; "L. J. Dawdy Report," in Work, *Re-Union*, 10–11; Capps, *Administrative History*, ch. 2; Corman, "Illinois Monument," 27–28; Work, *Re-Union*, 14; J. B. Work and S. W. Rilea, "Business Meeting, Col. Dan. McCook's Brigade," 15 May 1901, in Work, *Re-Union*, 137, 140–42; "J. B. Work Report," in Work, *Re-Union*, 12; "Kennesaw Memorial Association Perfects Its Organization," *Indianapolis Journal*, 11 August 1901.

66. Capps, *Administrative History*, ch. 2; Corman, "Illinois Monument," 28; Hess,

Introduction by Mark A. Smith

Kennesaw Mountain, 237; "An Act Making Appropriation for the Erection of a Monument on the Battlefield of Kenesaw Mountain, Georgia," 11 June 1911, in State of Illinois, *Laws of the State of Illinois, by the Forty-Seventh Assembly at the Regular Biennial Session Begun and Held at the Capitol, in the City of Springfield, on the Fourth Day of January A.D. 1911, and Adjourned Sine Die on the First Day of June, A.D. 1911* (Springfield: Illinois State Journal Company, 1911), 72.

67. "An Act Making Appropriation for the Erection of a Monument on the Battlefield of Kenesaw Mountain, Georgia," 11 June 1911, in State of Illinois, *Laws of the Forty-Seventh General Assembly*, 72–73, quotes from 72; Corman, "Illinois Monument," 28; Work, *Re-Union*, 14; J. B. Work and S. W. Rilea, "Business Meeting, Col. Dan. McCook's Brigade," 15 May 1901, in Work, *Re-Union*,140–42; P. J. Lucey to L. J. Dawdy, 21 January 1914, in "Kenesaw Monument Commission," in Patrick J. Lucey, *Biennial Report of the Opinions of the Attorney General of the State of Illinois* (Springfield: Illinois State Journal Company, 1914), 789.

68. Corman, "Illinois Monument," 28; Capps, *Administrative History*, ch. 2; Hess, *Kennesaw Mountain*, 237; Mark A. Smith, field visit to Kennesaw Mountain National Battlefield Park, 22 November 2017; "William G. Putney Recollection," in Work, *Re-Union*, 18.

69. Capps, *Administrative History*, ch. 2; Hess, *Kennesaw Mountain*, 237; Dunne's remarks quoted in Corman, "Illinois Monument," 29.

70. Corman, "Illinois Monument," 30; Holmes, "Movements and Positions," 65, 87–88.

71. Capps, *Administrative History*, ch. 2; Hess, *Kennesaw Mountain*, 238; Corman, "Illinois Monument," 26–30.

One

And now, while from my writings, one might cull a fairly full account of the movements and positions of the Third Brigade and its several regiments, from first to last of the Kenesaw affair of June 27–July 3, 1864, it is the purpose of this paper to record a somewhat connected sketch of the transactions on that occasion. There is no dispute, I think, about the point from which we started, or the date, June 27, 1864, or the hour, about 8:30 a.m. At this distance in time, it seems a strange entry for me to have made in my journal, on the memorable day, to wit:

> June 27. The charge. Let memory tell it later on, or let no more be said by the writer. *It was terrible.*

It was made in the trench on the morning of the 28th and I *suppose* the conditions were most unfavorable to writing history. The air was full of the odor of blood and powder and fresh earth and wounds and death. In the phrase, "or let no more be said by the writer," is the breath of absolute uncertainty of life on that hillside—any moment might bring a close to any life. If a time should ever come, as it did, when I could write a description, it might be written; if not, then the three underscored words should paint all the picture, then so vivid in my mind and memory, less than twenty-four hours old, "It was terrible." In case I should not be spared to do such further writing, there was the reflection that history, written in reports and by comrades, then and in later times, would make record of the day's work and my omission and future silence would not affect results.

It is vain, I know, but now I wish I had written everything possible to be "put down in writing" that day and the days following, as to our then current experiences and observations. That is "spilled milk."

Movements and Positions in the Battle of Kennesaw Mountain

Speaking of odors on a preceding page, I am reminded of a fact which is probably recorded somewhere in my books or letters. I wore light flannel underclothes into that charge. It was impossible to make changes—practically impossible—until the morning of July 3, next ensuing. That underclothing became impregnated with the stench of odors of the surrounding atmosphere and seemed to hold them "in solution." This was in addition to the perspiration, sensible and insensible, of the body from which they were not taken, either day or night. All in all, it was not the odor of "the great unwashed," but of the charnel house, which now and then would come up between my neck and the permanent collar of that battle shirt. I tell things as they were; there was no shame in them; they were a part of horrid war. The bath-room, the ward-robe, the drawing-room, the parlor, the dining-room and kitchen were an open trench in Georgia clay and gravel!

The entries immediately following the one just quoted from my journal are as follows:

> June 28. Behind works close to *Johnny*; say forty yards distant.
> June 28, 29, and 30. A constant *pouring* of rifle balls. Some casualties.
> July 1. As for the three preceding days.
> July 2. Lieutenant Miser, Company G, wounded. Midnight: Enemy evacuate their works, fearful of a mine of powder springing under their feet on the 4th, and it *might have been*.

Looking over the ground from our breastworks, not by an open and free survey, at leisure, but by a glance under a headlog, which skimmed the surface of the ground, only, I overestimated the distance by twenty feet, or a little more, to the enemy's line, that next morning.

Note that on the 28th the 52d was in the *front* line and *next* to "*Johnny's*" works, as we called him, in those days.

The conditions were sized up exactly by the two phrases written on the 30th, and which tersely epitomized three days of deadly work. At the end of two more like them, the 52d could count twenty five men killed and wounded, in addition to the eighty three who had fallen in the direct assault of the 27th. It was on the 3d of July and after we reached those "woods" that the entry of July 2d was made. Very clearly as early in life as that date, I was familiar with Maud Muller's "might have been."

Chapter One

Now, to the review:

It will not be necessary here to repeat the statements of fact, or any of them set forth in the New Alexandria Address on Kenesaw, August 20, 1897, "Then and Now," 171–201[1]; a copy is set out at the close of this book (Appendix). When the assault failed—I mean at the moment when all thought of going over the rebel works was abandoned—the left wing of the 52d Ohio, my special charge,[2] and with, and in, which I had moved from the top of the hill, six hundred yards away, was in line, and, while it had suffered heavily in killed and wounded, *was unbroken*. The same thing could not truthfully be said of any other regiment, or half regiment, in the Third Brigade. Going up through the woods, after passing the rebel rifle pits, at the edge of the timber, and when we were well up to the slight crest—not then apparent to us, but along which our line was afterward built—we met a tide of retreating men of two classes: 1, wounded, and 2, utterly demoralized. They came like a wave, in a mass—somewhat confused—striking the right wing of the 52d a sort of glancing blow, i.e, glancing off to the right, breaking companies A, F, D and I, to the rear, more or less, and very considerably confusing the extreme right companies for a little time. The alignment of a regiment in those days was this, looking to the front with arrows:

```
         ↑                    ↑                    ↑
Left    B    G    K    E    H    C    I    D    F    A    Right
```

Such was the drill and discipline of the 52d, however, that its right wing recovered largely from the break thus caused and passed the crest in a fair alignment, and it moved on until within from fifty to seventy feet of the enemy's breastworks—the left wing a little nearer than the right, because of the shape of the rebel line—where it lay down flat upon the ground. I heard no order to halt or lie down; I think no order will disclose who was, at that moment, in command of the brigade. I have no doubt that McCook had fallen and was being carried back, but I saw nothing of either event, as his place and mine were separated by more than the length of a regiment—the bias of the whole brigade, from right front to left rear,

Movements and Positions in the Battle of Kennesaw Mountain

as then organized—and the smoke of battle, at that point, would cut off a much shorter view.

```
    85 Ill.        Deployed as | skirmishers.
                   ————————————|————————————
    125 Ill.       ————————————|————————————
    86 Ill.        ————————————|————————————
    22 Ill.        ————————————|————————————
    52 Ohio.       ————————————|————————————
```

The lying down of the 52d was a spontaneous movement. It had never been drilled in retreat; it could go up on the dead wall, which was insurmountable and there lie down, but it never understood going back without order. I had drilled and commanded it for many months, and its officers had its unwavering confidence. It had started from the top of the other hill, the last regiment in the column—there were four regiments in front of it, ten paces apart.

It had met other regiments in a tide of defeat as it went up the hill. It had passed the crest and it saw not one of its predecessors in the foreground, but that ground practically cleared all save dead and wounded. The four had melted away before a "withering fire" and eighty-three out of its own ranks had fallen, but it knew only its drill and its duty and its courage. Its drill kept it in line, even under a storm of rifle balls; its duty excluded the thought of retreat, without an order, and its courage was of soldierly sublimity. The unconscious thought of every man, as he grasped the situation and sank down was, "if four regiments have failed against this fire, the remnants of one cannot hope to carry the enemy's works," or, "words to that effect."

The 52d Ohio was, in the language of Gen. Jeff. C. Davis,[3] "the best drilled regiment in the 14th Army Corps," and that fact made it *stick* in line, on that fatal slope, and *save that day*.

I do not forget my own view as the boys sank to the earth. I was last down, taking in the situation over the heads of the line as it sank. There were no federal troops in front, or to the right or left, either moving or

Chapter One

standing or lying down, except the dead and wounded. Wounded men were endeavoring to get back singly and in pairs and many of them were shot down in the effort. This condition applied to the 52d, while we lay there. Lying close to the ground, a man would be shot. Instantly, he would, if only wounded, rise to his feet with the thought of help somewhere in the rear, among surgeons and hospitals. Exposed from head to feet another ball would end his days. It was sickening—a holy horror. I was in the left of the regiment and, going up, had passed just to the right of the big tree by which the tunnel was afterward started—a little to the left of it. How long we lay there, I think no man on earth can now tell, or could then have told, with accuracy. One thing, I think, is certain: we lay there long enough to make a rallying point for the boys of the first four regiments, who had gone up against as deadly a fire as entrenched infantry could deliver, in that day. By it, they had been driven back by, and through, the right of the 52d, as already described, but when they found that we had gone forward and not returned, they stopped between the crest and the edge of the woods and themselves lay down, in self defense. To stand up or walk or run down that hill was almost certain death, and so, according to my knowledge, as to part, and my impressions, as to other things, at that moment, referred to above, when the assault definitely failed, the situation was like this:

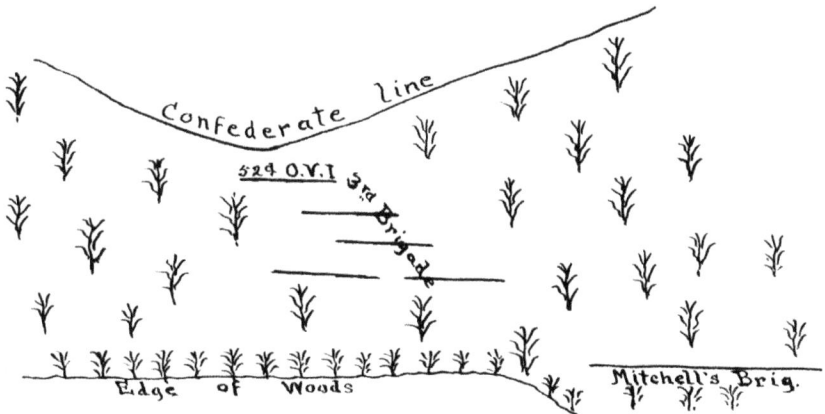

Movements and Positions in the Battle of Kennesaw Mountain

The four leading regiments, at the moment, were badly broken up and confused, but the mass of their men dropped and stayed on the hillside, in the wood, i.e, did not go back, either to Noyes Creek,[4] or the little open field, which we had crossed.

Let me state here what should probably have been stated above. The retreat of the other regiments, or rather, I should say, of parts of the other regiments, began before we entered the edge of the wood. It was more the rush of wounded men, for the guns of the enemy swept the ground and were effective from the time we crossed Noyes Creek and began to cross the little field, in which, about—a little more than—half way over, the regiments lay down. It has been said that there was no order for any such thing. The stop, so made, was very brief and we were up and forward; 52d men began falling as soon as we started forward. The soldiers who were retreating when we entered the wood, in the edge of which we passed the rebel rifle pits, had not reached the rebel works, or even the crest, before being wounded or turning back. As we lay in the little field, a perfect sheet of lead hurtled over-head, so that a comparatively compact body of 2400 to 2500 men, as the Third Brigade was, going up that slope, required very little marks-manship to kill and wound, and one ball might easily kill, or wound, more than one or two men.

The range was easy and fatal, and we were within it, as already stated, from the time we crossed the Creek.

The rush of men we met before we reached the crest was not the wounded alone; but no sentence of all this sketch must ever be understood as reflecting on the courage of any man, or company, or regiment, or officer, belonging to the Third Brigade. No such thing is intended.

In going up the slope the line was swerved slightly to the right, and when the rearward rush came, striking the right of the 52d, it had a tendency to change its direction by retarding and confusing the wing of the regiment a little. The result was that when we lay down in line—a thing which, of course, none of the other four regiments had done, or thought of doing, probably, the center of the regiment was somewhat to the right of the dead angle, or, in other words, the center of the dead angle and the center of the left wing of the 52d squarely confronted at that point.

Now, I come back to conditions at the moment of the failure, again. It would be utterly impossible for me to locate the lines of the other four

Chapter One

regiments, so far as they had lines; at that moment they were on that slope and in the woods, with wounded of all the regiments stretched back to, and beyond, the Creek and up the hill down which we had charged.

By the way, I never recrossed Noyes Creek, or went back a rod from our line or works after the charge. The four regiments were badly knocked to pieces, or, to put it in another form, badly jammed together. There was doubtless a nucleus, or shortened line about the commanding officers of each, which gradually increased from the time the assault failed. My impression as to location is that sketched above. None of them were over at the left of the ground where the 125th Ill. and the 22d Ind. afterward entrenched. That was intensely dangerous ground, without entrenchments—as much so as the ground over which Harker's Brigade charged a little further to the left. Men could not live on it, even lying down, such was the exposure to the fire of that portion of the rebel line against which Harker and, at least, the left of our Brigade as finally located, charged. I know as much about their positions today as I ever did.

Having described the line on which the 52d sank down in front of the rebel breastwork, and above what I have called the crest, especially described in my Kenesaw Address of August 1897, I take up that line again. How long we remained there, I'll never be able to say—my best guess is from one half an hour to an hour. Closely as the men lay to the ground, in loading and firing at our invisible enemies behind earthworks and protected by headlogs, every now and then, a man would show that he had been killed or wounded in the line by a rebel shot and it was patent that we could do little, or nothing, by way of retaliation. After a time—say thirty minutes, possibly longer—whether it was an order or an instinct, it may not be safe to say—I think it was not an order from any Brigade commander; I recall none—the 52d began to *craw-fish* to the protection of the almost invisible crest, which lay just behind them. From the rebel works, outward to the lying line, it was nearly level and so it was for twenty five or thirty feet behind us, but, at that distance, there was a slight dip which ran to the right rear from the rear of the left of the regiment like this[5]:

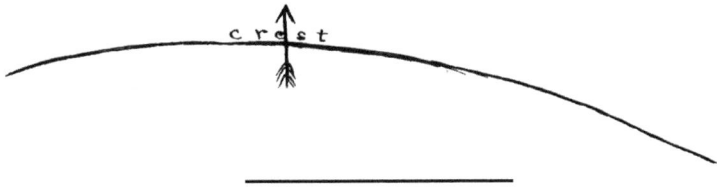

Movements and Positions in the Battle of Kennesaw Mountain

The crest was [still] there in 1897.

I mean that from this line a slight slope to the little field began and a man lying with his head at the line and his feet down the hill was just below the lowest line of fire from the rebel breast-works. It required close hugging of the ground to keep under their shots and I illustrated it at Richmond, in August 1901, as it was illustrated on the mountain side, by Capt. Rothacker's[6] old black hat, which they shot through the brim close down to his head as he lay flat on the earth, with his head on his crossed hands. I was lying, at the moment, with my head just above his knees and my body parallel with his on the left hand side of him as we looked to our front.

The boys crept back to this line gradually and held the ground, keeping up a steady fire on the headlogs in front. There were no picks, or spades, or shovels—nothing with which to fortify. Men could not live going down the slope and up the hill to the rear, down which hill and up which we had passed in making the charge. There was no such thing as going to the right or left under any kind of shelter and then to the rear in safety. And, besides, everybody was catching breath after the appalling scenes he had witnessed and was reminded that he might, each instant, become a skeleton, as he witnessed comrades becoming as the minutes and the hours went by. How long we lay at that crest, I do not know. Men of the Brigade, other regiments, crept to that line, on our right—none on our left; that was fatal ground then. After a while—after the noon hour, in one of the lulls of firing—for we were objects of attention not only by the breastworks fellows in front of us, but Carter's battery[7] to our right was pumping shot and shell at us steadily; the ridge, the crest, was slight protection against the artillery, too—an order came to move the regiment to the right and rear; this was the first order from Col. Dilworth[8] to myself as commander of the 52d O.V.I.[9] If I was on the ground, I could point out the exact line, but should say it was eight, possibly one hundred feet, from the position to which we had craw-fished at the crest. The 52d was still on the front line. While we were lying in this second, or rather, third position, other regiments of the Brigade lay to our left and partly in our rear—possibly one on the right, which had moved to the right rear with us, having crept gradually to the line of the crest on our right rear. I should say this last mentioned was the 85th Ill, in fact, I am sure of it. This posi-

Chapter One

tion was still in the woods, and while we were lying there a shot or shell from the Carter battery knocked from the limb of an oak tree just above me a fragment of the limb, which gave me a numbing blow on the back of the left wrist, but did not break the skin. As we lay here about, or a little before 4 p.m, when the firing died down, at one time, Lt. Col. Clancy made his appearance, coming down from where the right of the regiment had lain down above the crest. The distance back to the crest from the right of the regiment was greater than from the left, and such had been the danger, where he lay, that he preferred to lie still through the day and be taken for a dead man to making movement and being a dead one in fact, or being made prisoner. Working back cautiously, he finally succeeded in eluding the vigilance of the rebel riflemen and came down the hill. We had not known whether he was among the dead or wounded and when he appeared, safe and sound, the boys applauded to the peril of drawing the enemy's fire upon him before he dropped into the line out of range.

Quite soon after he came in, the regiment was ordered back to its original crest position and the boys, having thought over the situation and pulled themselves together, began to fortify. I can see the creeping up the hill and to the left again as if I was there, and in it, now. The 85th crept up with us on our right, keeping to the slightly refused crest.

The position which we left was not as far down as the line Mitchell's brigade fortified later; the position to which we returned and which the boys began to fortify was the first one we took at the crest, except that we extended it to the left when night came down, perhaps, thirty feet, or more, and pushed it a little further front—say a matter of ten or fifteen feet.

While we lay down the hill to the right, there were no troops to our left front or in our first position at the crest to which we had *craw-fished*. When Clancy came back, he came first to the 52d. At our right, both slightly in advance and in rear of our line extended, while we were so dropped back the 80 feet, lay regiments of Mitchell's brigade. Our line lay with the left advanced; no regiment lay as far advanced as our left. Other regiments of the Third Brigade lay to our left and left rear. There was not much order and the space occupied by our brigade was not very considerable. It is not accurate to say the regiments were huddled together, and yet, in a sense, that was the condition during a portion of the afternoon.

Movements and Positions in the Battle of Kennesaw Mountain

The Illinois regiments were reorganizing under fire. The 52d was never out of line, or in need of reorganization. When we moved up to the crest in front of the dead angle, the boys began fortifying in the manner described in the Kenesaw address, with bayonets for picks and tin plates and cups for shovels, and so on. By night-fall, they had quite a little trench and row of earth and *debris* on the upper side of it. The "breastwork" was not breast high then, but the accumulations on the upper side of the ditch, by the time night came down, were 18 inches to two feet high. The left of the regiment did not, during daylight, extend beyond my big oak tree, but as soon as it was dark so that picks and shovels could be brought down from the rear, with safety to the carriers, the 52d took position with its left beyond that tree to and covering the point where the tunnel was later opened and, on the regimental line, the breastworks grew apace. The men worked until away into the night, perhaps 2 o'clock, by which time the line was a protection against rifle balls and had headlogs on considerable portions of it. So, I account for the movements and positions of the 52d down to the morning of the 28th of June 1864.

The positions of the 85th Ill. from the time we dropped back to the crest on the 27th were these, substantially: It joined the 52nd and rallied up from the rear on its right as the 52d lay at the crest the first time and so remained until the movement of the 52d line to the right and rear, almost along the crest, down toward what was later the fortified position of Mitchell's brigade—to this movement the 85th conformed—and when we moved back up to the original crest position, the 85th moved with us into its former position and through the night of the 27–28, fortified its line in connection with that of the 52d, and this connecting position it occupied on the morning of the 28th. The movement of the 52d say twenty-five to thirty feet to the left, with part of its left wing beyond the big tree, when the tools came, at night fall, drew the 85th correspondingly to the left. It was, after nightfall, aligned a little further to the front that it had been in daylight, thus:

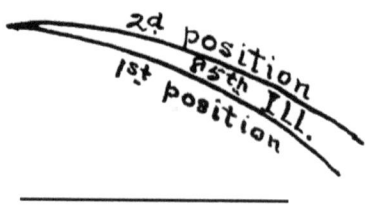

Chapter One

This was the movement on its part corresponding with the advance of 10 or 15 feet to the front by the 52d above mentioned. The reason for the advance was this: During the day we were obliged to lie below the crest for protection; correct engineering placed our breastworks *on the crest*.

While the 52d lay at the crest the first time, the 125th Ill. lay almost directly behind it down the hill and about in line with the position where Mitchell, later, intrenched, and it remained in that position until dusk and the tools came, when it moved to the position on the left of the 52nd with its right joined on to our left, near the present tunnel mouth, and its line extending down the hill to the left refused, like this:

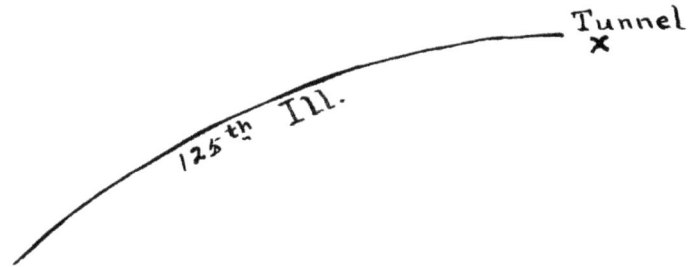

This position it fortified through the night of the 27–28. As already stated, this line was so exposed that men, unprotected by earthworks, could not live on it in daylight. The enemy in the breastworks against which Harker's brigade had charged could sweep the line with their guns *down to the ground*. This was true of the stretch of rebel works from the dead angle up along their line to the redoubt, where they had artillery, and beyond, on our left as we faced the enemy. Troops behind the angle and even north of the point could do execution along the ground before it was fortified. By morning, the 125th was, like the 52d and the 85th, well under cover of gravelly red clay, in the form of ditch and earthworks; and here was the 125th on the morning of the 28th.

The 22nd Ind, from its rallying position in the rear, while the 52d lay first at the crest, probably a little to the left and rear of the 125th, at least, in rear of it, moved with the latter, at dusk, and took position in rear of the left of the 125th and moved directly facing the left portion of the dead

Movements and Positions in the Battle of Kennesaw Mountain

angle, substantially parallel with the position of the 52d—which was, as stated at the right of the 125th—at the crest, like this:

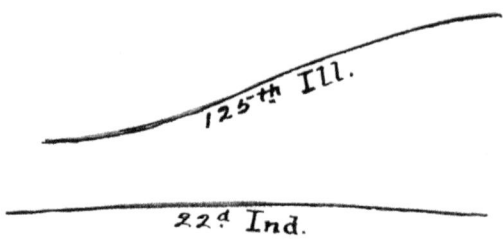

The 22d went into the ground, like the other, between sundown and daylight of 27–28th.

The 86th occupied a position at the right, behind the 85th, corresponding with that of the 22d at the left behind the 125th. It was wicked, deadly work all through the 28th and every now and then some poor fellow would fall even behind our dirt defenses. The artillery kept the trees above us badly disturbed, in a sort of quiver. There was great uncertainty in the minds of men in each line, querying as to whether a sally to break the opposite line was a possibility.

Some work was done with picks and shovels, strengthening our line, through the day and the work completed and the remainder of the headlogs were mounted that night. The rear lines, 22d and 86th, had no headlogs—they did not need them, as the works of their comrades cut off effective firing by those regiments and they needed protection only. The works on the ground today will confirm the positions taken, if they have not been destroyed since May 22d, 1897. Debate and dispute may arise and be maintained as to the position of any given regiment, at any given time, and the officers and men of each regiment *ought to know and remember* substantially the movements and positions of their own regiments, severally. As to the positions and movements of the 52d, I am as clear in my recollection as I was July 4th 1864. As to the positions of the 125th and the 22d, on our left, I am equally clear. As to whether or not there was a change or shift in the positions of the 85th and 86th between the night of the 27th and the night of July 2d, I am not absolutely clear. My position in the trench was with the left wing of the 52d and that specially

Chapter One

impressed the 125th and the 22nd on my mind, because not only every hour, but every moment we were in a sort of elbow-touch with, and in daylight in continual sight of, them. A shift between the 85th and 86th might have occurred without my having notice of it in the night and I might have forgotten, if I once knew, but I have no recollection of any break in the line where the 52d and the 85th joined. And these positions were maintained until the Johnnies went away on the night of July 2d and gave us both lines of breastworks at daylight, July 3, 1864.

This is a transcript from my memory unaided by any effort to find, or know, what others may have said or recollected on the points. My journal entries, made on the spot, brief and unsatisfactory as they may appear are to my mind suggestive and confirmatory of the work of simple memory.

And now, this paper shall have two other branches, so to speak: first, the observations which may occur to mind upon a careful reading of the sketch down to this point, and, secondly, in course of time, a discussion of other and different views of my comrades which have already, or may hereafter, come to me.

As to the first.

I have suggested that there is no dispute about the date and place of the charge, because from what has already come to me on the subject and on other subjects connected with Kenesaw, there will be much dispute among survivors touching regimental movements and positions. It is not sarcasm to say there is no dispute about time and place, for I opine that almost all else will be a matter of difference, after these nearly forty years.

Men are not gods to know and remember always and as their faces and forms differ and change with time, so must their memories, more or less, grow apart, and may do so honestly.

I wrote that I *supposed* the conditions were not favorable to writing history in the trench on the morning of June 28th, 1864. That was sarcasm, for I know, even now, that conditions were most unfavorable. If one had held his hand above a headlog there for the space of three minutes, with the palm open toward the dead angle, it would have been shot through as surely as the owner lived, and it might have been done before ten seconds went by after the exposure, so keen-eyed were the marksmen, in each line, at the point in question.

Movements and Positions in the Battle of Kennesaw Mountain

Lieutenant Miser's wound was mortal; he died at his home, August 2d, next ensuing.[10] At Richmond, Aug. 8th, 1901, I commented on the fact that he and grandfather's Lieut. Col. John Andrews, 3rd Regt. Ohio Militia, in the war of 1812, are buried at the same little town, Salem, Jefferson County, Ohio.

The mine which was being prepared for the 4th of July was a very small factor in bringing about the evacuation of the rebel works, if it had any influence whatever. The line on Kenesaw had become untenable, because our troops were pressing past the rebel left and the enemy was simply flanked out of the position, as he should have been without the awful sacrifice of June 27th, 1864.[11]

No doubt the mine would have been ready to spring under the angle and would have been fired by July 4th, a sort of celebration. The boys were so quietly talking about it among themselves from the time the tunnel was started. The sharp eyes of the rebels were not long detecting what was going on, after the tunnel was started, on the morning of the 29th, though I think they did not do so until after the truce was over, perhaps not until the 30th.

It must be remembered that I am not writing a history of the assault of June 27th, 1864, but am endeavoring to put down on my record a transcript from my memory of the *movements* and *positions*—the tactical history—of the five regiments of the Third Brigade from the morning of the 27th of June to the morning of the 3rd of July 1864.

A controversy is coming, or on even now, among survivors on the subject and that has stirred me to do this work for my private record, which should have been done long ago, but, "better late than never."

I do not intend to enter the lists of disputants, at any point of time, or space. As I wrote a correspondent, on the 16th Nov, '03. I am putting it down "for my boy" if he should ever care, or have use, for it. So much and such of the other events of the assault as may throw light on these movements and positions have been, or will be, freely used in completing this sketch.

Speaking of lying down when we were partly across the little field, I am reminded that the statement has somewhere been made, in recent years, that it was never known how such thing happened, or whence such order emanated, if one was given, for such movement. The statement was

Chapter One

further made that the regiments in front, or some of them, did not lie down or halt; and these things were said in explanation of failure of the assault, to show that the blow intended to be delivered was weakened by taking from the force of the impact against the enemy, the momentum of the rear regiments, which had lain down and so been left in rear by those in front marching against the works, leaving the others to come up later and deliver a second portion of a divide blow.

These statements may be in Mr. Work's little book on Kenesaw[12]—I am not now certain where I saw them. They were new to me. I had always supposed and believed that the whole brigade lay down at the time the 52d and the 22d and the 86th did so. I so suppose and believe yet, and am unable to comprehend how the 85th and the 125th could have gone on while we lay in the little field. They did not do so.

    1. We should have seen them going up the hill, certainly, a thing we did not see.

    2. We should have felt their fearful repulse in a different way and place and time, it seems to me, if such a separation had occurred.

    3. We should have known, or heard, something of it before the business at the dead angle was ended.

I *supposed* then, and have always since supposed, that an intelligent order had been given, either by the commander of the division, or by the commander of the brigade, for the halt and rest; and my further understanding has always been that such order was not given until the men had moved in column of assault, at a slow double quick, fully 400 yards and were found to be, as they were, in fact, winded by the exertion. The thing ought to have been thought of before we started, but it seems that it was not, and men were expected to double quick, in that way, in that heat, in brigade column, 300 yards down slope and 300 yards up slope and strike such fortifications with all their breath and all their strength as full and fresh as at the start, when, in truth, and, in fact, such a run was calculated, made at an unbroken pace, to exhaust most men, and utterly wind them before their fighting time and ground could be reached.

Well, I always supposed and believed that the halt and rest, in the little field, were to enable the panting men to catch their breath preparatory to the upward assault upon the works, which lay 200 yards above

Movements and Positions in the Battle of Kennesaw Mountain

them, at the top of the slope. The halt and rest were needed and full of good hard sense; even if no order was made, the men were justified in taking them, without orders.

There may have been no order; I can easily believe there was none; I am sure I heard none, except it may have been repetition of the words "lie down" from the lips of the men near me.

I have referred to the effect of the scenes through which we had passed down to the definite failure of the charge. It was of a stunning, sense-benumbing character. Almost 25 percent of the officers and men in the charging column had gone down, killed or wounded—a bloody picture. Two commanders of the brigade, McCook and Harmon, were gone.[13] Harker on our left and Shane on our right killed, were officers of other brigades, but known to, and held in high esteem by, the Third.[14] The brotherhood of the Third had great gaps in it and the sorrows of kinship were not wanting. The veil and burden of a soldierly grief were over every mind and upon and about every heart—it was poor human nature, nay, rich human nature, a testimonial to its solemn, sincere depth and sympathy, even in circumstances of deadly peril.

It must be remembered, too, that there was added to it all the depression, which resulted from the first impression that we had sustained bitter defeat. None saw at first what appeared later, one of the most unique situations in the history of warfare, ancient or modern. It was not settled and no man could foresee, on the 27th of June, that we should hold that immortal, bloody ground, though we had not carried the enemy's fortifications. With the lapse of the hours and particularly of the night of the 27th and its work, an appreciation of the feat of the Third Brigade grew in all minds and the confidence in its strength and courage to hold "Key Point," as our boys christened it, grew and grew even unto the end, which fastened in history the immortality of that achievement.

Doubtless, the mental operations and conditions of men differed, but, I am sure, that I have stated the "consensus" of mental conditions on the general points mentioned.

I have probably not stated in definite terms what was true, and if I had done so it will bear repetition, i.e, the first fortifying the 52d boys did, and they were first of all to do it, was after they moved back up the slope to their first crest position, and this movement, be it understood, was along the line

Chapter One

on which the breastworks were constructed that afternoon and night. It was a simple moving back to the former position by creeping up left and front. It was at that point, in time and place, that the thought of *staying there* had most diminutive birth. The birth may have seemed premature and doubtful, but when the boys began to push their bayonets into the earth to loosen it and to reach back for their cups and plates to scoop and throw it up toward the rebels, there was the thought of staying there, and when they stooped behind formidable earthworks next morning, the premature birth mentioned was taken out of cotton and clothed in infantry blue.

The impression must not be taken that any of Mitchell's regiments, at any time, lay in front of the 52d or the 85th. What I intended, at the point, where the subject is mentioned, was to say that one or two of Mitchell's regiments, when we lay, for a time, down the hill and to our right, *may have lain* in front of our line extended thus:

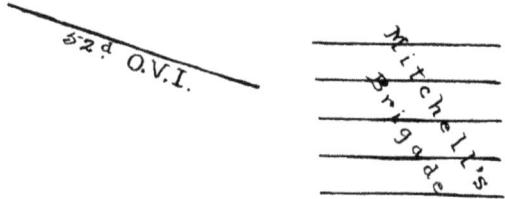

I am not right certain about any of them being in front of that "line extended"; I think none was. While we lay there, some parts of the regiments of our brigade, lying on our left, were nearly as far front as the 52d.

My memory of positions when the 52d dropped back from the crest to the right and rear is, in substance, this:

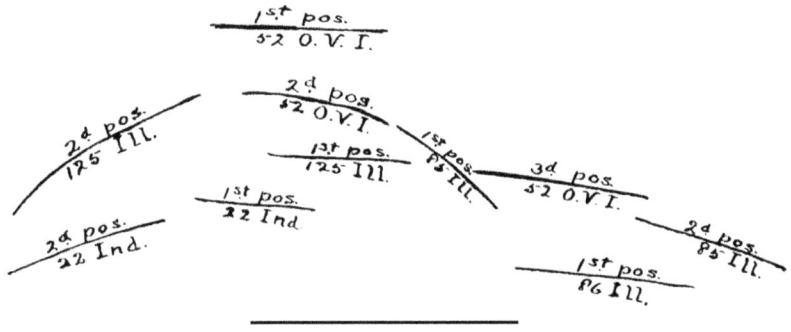

Movements and Positions in the Battle of Kennesaw Mountain

The moves from these final positions and fortifications are made sufficiently clear in the foregoing text. The forgoing sketch strings out the right rear a little too far to express my idea, but is only a little out of proportion in that respect. All were in the woods.

One starts down a long steep stairway; something happens near the upper step and then an hundred things happen to the falling, bumping, bewildered man, or woman, or child, and at the bottom, in a heap, the victim is as able to give all the details, with accuracy, as the officer or soldier, who goes through such a charge as Kenesaw. Things happen with wonderful rapidity; some are known; some are partially known; some are unknown to the participant. The victim of such a fall can safely say there was a fall, but its details, in all their detail, he never can remember and state; he never knew them all.

And, so, I come, at last, to condense my memories with my pen thus:

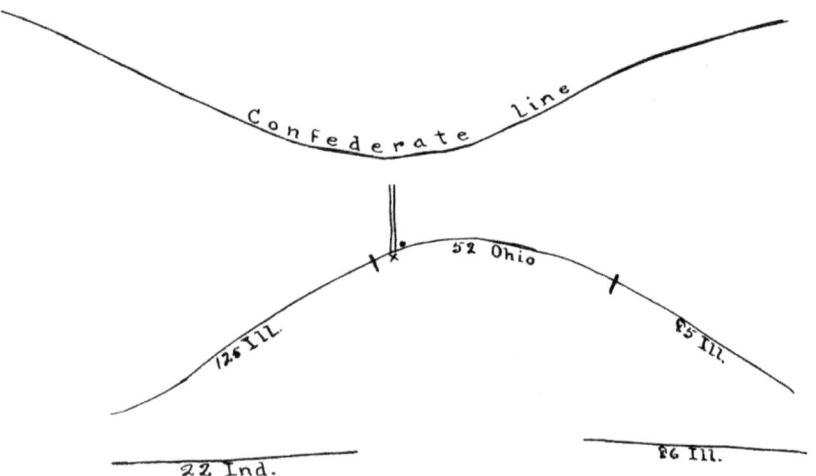

Commencing with the night of the 27th June and ending with the night of the 2d July 1864.

These marks, the penmanship of war, are on the ground to this day. It scarecely seems seven years since I saw and walked over them all.

Another suggestion should probably be made before closing this branch of the supplemental observations, and that is that a good many state-

Chapter One

ments touching the assault of June 27th, 1864, may be found in my writings, which may shed additional light on its character and facts as viewed from my standpoint; most of them, perhaps, in the record of my private correspondence and records as distinguished from the professional, since the beginning of the year 1900, but there are some before that, all the way back to 1864.[15] Nowhere, however, have I made any such paper as this, or anything like it, for comprehensive detail, touching the movements and positions of brigade and regiments during the Kenesaw days and nights.

I do not write with any feeling that there can be no error in what is written; nor do I write with any purpose to prejudice any officer, man, company, or regiment, of the Third Brigade. As Schley said at Santiago, there was "glory enough for all,"[16] and the truth, the whole truth, and nothing but the truth, should be the sole aim of one writing for the present generation, or, as I am doing, for later generations, on this greatest of the little battles of the Civil War. It was remarkable and the Work brochure is one of the most important memorials so far produced touching many of its features.[17]

On page 56 *supra* is reference to the return of Clancy to the regiment from above the crest. I see that thing as though it had occurred today. There was no soldier of another regiment between him and the 52d—lying in line—when he crept over the crest and down the slope a little ways and then rose to his feet and walked into the line of the 52d.[18] I know whereof I affirm:

    a. Davis was too good a soldier to pass Col. Dilworth, as the brigade commander, who had acquitted himself with honor, to ask a *regimental* commander for a report involving the conduct of the *brigade.*[19]

    b. Clancy would have been guilty of an assumption, which the facts at no time warranted, if he had sent word to the division commander, past the brigade commander, or through the brigade commander, that a regiment in the brigade *proposed to hold* the front line, or the rear line. If he had known, or, if he knew, anything about the brigade, or its movements, or positions, or the movements, or positions, of its several regiments, he knew that they were subject to Col. Dilworth's orders and liable to shift and change of position, at any moment.

    c. When Clancy rejoined the regiment and could have sent any word to Davis, it was untrue that the 52d was distinguished as holding the front line alone. The 125th was practically on the front line to its left and the 85th was, in like relation, on its right.

Movements and Positions in the Battle of Kennesaw Mountain

It hardly makes the letter d, but men were not running much back and forth between the time the assault failed and nightfall. The ground over which they must pass was so completely covered by the guns of the enemy that an insurance company would not have placed a policy on the passer's life at a premium of 100 cents on the dollar; for that would have been to lose the expense and labor of doing the business, so far as the ground between the Third Brigade and Davis' Head Quarters was concerned.

[e.] As we have seen and as we all knew to our sorrow, not a pick or a shovel could be, or was, brought to us until sundown, as dangerous was every line of approach to us from the rear, while daylight lasted.

My conclusion on this subject is the one stated in the text above: *Davis never sent such query to Clancy and Clancy never sent such answer to Davis.*

Another suggestion, which is well-nigh obvious, might be made in support of the conclusion just repeated and that is that:

f. I was in command of the 52d regiment during the time such query and answer would likely have occurred, if ever, and no such question was asked or answer given while I was so in command, on that line. Dilworth had, as Brigade commander, sent me orders as regimental commander.

g. One more suggestion is made, somewhat personal and argumentative in its nature. I *never heard of the alleged question and answer until Sam. Grimshaw communicated them to Mr. Work and the latter stated them to me, a few months ago.* It seems rational to suppose that if such a thing occurred some knowledge or information about it would somehow have reached me before the lapse of more than an ordinary lifetime. *I was not away from the 52d from January 1863, until June 1865,* and in that time was in command of it more than sixteen months.

As to Henry J. Aten's—85th—impression that no second line of the brigade was established, or fortified, until after the truce of the 29th, to bury the dead between the lines, I am very certain it is erroneous.[20] The 22d Indiana moved to the left and rear of the 125th Ill. at nightfall of the 27th and went into the ground just as the 125th did from our left down the slope. The impression is erroneous. Every line of the brigade was fixed and fortified before the flag of truce for the burial of the dead between the lines. It was on the 2d of July that 1st Lieut. Dave Miser rose up in Company G, 52d, not far from my big tree, and started down the hill in

Chapter One

rear of the line of the 125th Ill, directly toward the line of the 22d Ind., which he had nearly reached when he was wounded by a shot from the enemy's line. As he started down the hill, some of the boys cautioned him to stoop so as to have the protection of the works, but the stout spirited fellow said that he would "stoop to no d——d rebel." He paid the penalty with his life. I never quite understood why "Dave" did it. For nearly six days and nights every man on the slope—"Dave" Miser among them—had known the death-risk in standing or walking anywhere on that slope above the protection of our earthworks in daylight. He failed to appreciate the constant danger and as time passed grew, perhaps, to despise it.

I do not gather clearly what Aten means in a letter written me the other day, in which he refers to "the advanced or second line."[21] He must have helped to build and hold the only line of the 85th Ill. on that ground. There was no line in front, except a rifle pit, mentioned in one of my recent letters to him, out in advance, large enough to hold ten, possibly twenty, men—I really think not so many—which was occupied at night, only, to guard against surprise. It was not occupied at all during the last three nights. The memories of some clear-headed men were clouded by the intensity of *life* and *death* at Kenesaw from the beginning of the assault to the close of the siege. It was intense in each sense and I do not wonder at the departures in the testimony after forty years, even throwing aside the sway of interest and passion.

Next comes the official report of Col. Langley, touching the engagement.[22] He and his Colonel, Oscar F. Harmon, did not agree very well from their entry into service and quite soon therafter Langley was detailed on Staff Duty with Gen. John M. Palmer.[23] This position he continued to fill until *after* the Kenesaw assault, when the death of Harmon opened the way for, and seemed to require, Langley's return to the 125th and so he came back while we were still in line in front of the "dead angle" on Kenesaw. At this time, and until the close of the battle of Jonesboro, Georgia, September 1st, 1864, Col. Dilworth[24] of the 85th Illinois was in command of the brigade. Dilworth was wounded at Jonesboro and thenceforward Col. Langley was in command of the brigade until Fearing was placed in charge at the opening of the Carolina Campaign of Savannah, Georgia.

Movements and Positions in the Battle of Kennesaw Mountain

Gen. Fearing was wounded at Bentonville, North Carolina, and so Langley was again in command of the brigade, which he retained until muster out at Washington, D.C. Fearing lost a thumb at Bentonville.[25]

Col. Langley's report of the Atlanta Campaign is found in War Records, Vol. 72, pp. 708–716. The report of the Kenesaw assault commences just below the middle of page 710 and ends at a point a little nearer the bottom of page 711.

It will not pay to copy it here.[26] It will be all I care, or need, to do to point out *some of the errors* into which Col. Langley inadvertently fell in making up this portion of his report. My criticisms have no element of feeling or resentment of any kind in them for the Colonel and myself are on very friendly terms, personally, but while the errors may not be large, or important, they are corrected in the interest of truth and justice—of accurate history.

1. It is not "a little more than half a mile" from the point where dispositions were made to the works to be stormed. It is about 600 yards—Captain Work's map shows the exact distance.[27] A half a mile would be 880—almost 900—yards. Work's map shows the distance by actual measurement as 1377 feet; down to the creek, 675; across the little field, 372; up to our works, 225; thence to the Confederate works, 105. Restated in another form: down to the creek, 225 yards; from the creek to the rebel works, 231 yards, making a total of 456 yards.

2. The abrupt hill and the thickly matted vines down at the creek were practical figments. The alleged marshy character of the creek was not worthy of notice. None of these three items mentioned in the report really had a potential existence; not a step was broken by either, except the little bank down into the creek. No confusion resulted from either, not an atom of it.

3. There was no turning of faces to the enemy, for none were, down to that time, turned away from the enemy.

4. The edge of the field where we entered the wood, going up the hill, was—not fifteen rods, but—more than twice fifteen rods from "the point of attack."

5. Col. Harmon had been dead some time before any lines were "reformed" a few steps in the rear and partially under the crest of the hill. When Col. Harmon fell, the 52d Ohio was in line unbroken, except,

Chapter One

as described, at the right, above the crest moving forward on the works and, at the distance heretofore described, lay down in line and remained there for the time indicated in the preceding pages.

The colonel is off with reference to Dilworth's order and the works at sixty yards. It was safe to say they did not exceed sixty yards, for they did not exceed thirty-three!

He is mistaken about the "well sheltered by works" by 3 p.m. "Not by a large majority."

I have stated the facts above. It was not and it is not true.

Langley brings himself on the ground at 4 *p.m.* He came back that afternoon, I remember, and about the hour he specifies. I saw his arrival.

Now, I quote from page 711 of the 72 W. R.:

> After the confusion [note that word confusion] of battle was over, the brigade was disposed thus; The Eighty-fifth Illinois on the right, connecting with the Second Brigade; the Twenty-second Indiana on the left, connecting with General Harker's brigade; the One hundred and twenty-fifth Illinois in the center, and the Eighty-Sixth Illinois and Fifty-second Ohio in reserve, the lines remaining the same until the morning of the 28th, when the One hundred and twenty-fifth was relieved by the Eighty-sixth Illinois; that in turn was relieved on the morning of the 29th by the Fifty-second Ohio.

He says the truce to bury or remove the dead between the lines occurred on the 29th; then he adds: "On the 30th a new line of works was constructed within from five to seven rods of the enemy's line." Then he mentions the gun-glasses.

Now, in the matter quoted, the Colonel is *full of inaccuracy.*

My sketch, while not written in refutation, shows where Langley goes wrong on these points:

The 52d never was in reserve at Kenesaw. It held the center on the same line—the line of works—which it built, from the afternoon of June 27th, when it crept up to it, until the morning of July 3d. It is useless to tell me or any of my men who were there, any other story. I have sketched the positions of the regiments and there they must remain while truth remains.

The man does not, never did, live who could or can point out a rear or a reserved line occupied by the 52d Ohio at Kenesaw. It never did occupy such line after it passed the other regiments and sank to the ground

Movements and Positions in the Battle of Kennesaw Mountain

in line within seventy feet of the Confederate breastworks at the end of the charge.

Captain Samuel Rothacker's hat—Co. G, 52d—is in his Doctor office in Richmond, Ohio, today with the hole through its brim, down close to the band, and the rebel who shot it didn't miss the back of the Captain's head a quarter of an inch, as the latter lay with his forehead on his crossed hands and the hands on the ground, at that crest, near that big tree, after the 52d moved backward to the crest. That shot was fired and that hole was made before the boys had made even a little furrow in the ground with their bayonets and tin pans and cups, as a beginning of fortifications. The 52d made two other moves before it broke ground to fortify.

The old black hat in Richmond, and I had it in my hand the other day—August 1901—is a silent witness that I am not mistaken and Langley is in error as to the position of the 52d O.V.I. I was then commanding that regiment, witnessed that shot, at that instant lay with my head at the Captain's knee, behind him on the slope.

The new line of June 30th is pure imagination. The line was fixed before night-fall on the 27th, fortified that night and stands in the same place today.

The 52d Ohio occupied the front center of the Third Brigade, fortified and held it from start to finish.

No such changes of its line as Langley describes ever occurred.

Through all those days I thought the 125th Illinois joined us on our left; certainly did on the night of the 27th of June and onward until Lieut. Dave Miser—G, 52d—fell mortally wounded *just behind the left of the 125th line* of July 2d.

If any other regiment took its place the afternoon of July 2d I have *clear* forgotten it. The 125th boys were working with the 52d boys on the tunnel all through the 2d of July.

My place was near the left of the 52d in a sort of contact with the 125th. It was this fact which made me say that a shift might possibly have occurred between the 85th and the 86th, at the right of the 52d without my noting it—after night. Such a thing could not have occurred with the 125th and any other regiment without my knowledge.

Harker's brigade did not stay in the bottom or on the slope and fortify; it couldn't live there and the 22d Indiana never connected with it there.

Chapter One

There are no earthworks and there never were, nor any other kind of works, on the left of the 22d Indiana line of earthworks, or on the left of the 125th Illinois there.

During what may properly be called the siege, my place was, as already stated, with the left wing of the 52d and that fact brought me in close contact continually with the officers and men of my old company, G. Rothacker was its Captain and Miser was its lieutenant.

Against the theory advanced by some members of the brigade in "modern times" that the 52d ever occupied a second line of breastworks, or that there was a line of earthworks occupied by our men in front of us, at any time, I have told this story:

A very little to the right of the tunnel opening, directly *in the line* of the 52d works, in the left wing of the regiment, stood a large tree. The headlog on top of the earthworks, under which our men fired, rested against the tree *inside*, speaking with reference to our line of works. On the 29th or 30th of June—I am not certain which, though inclined to think it was the 30th—I borrowed a Henry rifle from one of my men—it was the only one in the regiment—and climbing cautiously up behind the big tree, which, properly used, made a complete shield for my tall, slender body, I stood on the headlog and began annoying the Confederate line on our left by an enfilading fire. The elevated position gave me a line of fire against which the traverses of the enemy were not entirely proof when used in the ordinary way, i.e, my shots had a slight plunge, which made it necessary for the other fellows to keep closer to the bottom of the traverses and the works.

I became deeply interested in my work. At that time, if a soldier wished a hole through his black hat, all he had to do was to raise it slowly on a ramrod, or the point of a bayonet, above the headlog a little way, and then slowly lower it; he was sure to find bullet holes in it when he took it off the point. Well, as I have just stated, I became much interested in the work and the "fun" I was having with the Henry and for a moment forgot the size of that tree. In this instant of forgetfulness, I happened to turn my eyes past the right side of the tree when I discovered my whole head and right shoulder in full view of the Confederate angle, directly in front of our works and of the long stretch of rebel breastworks running off to our right. The discovery sent a cold chill all over me. No man ever changed

Movements and Positions in the Battle of Kennesaw Mountain

his position more quickly than I dropped down among the boys, glad to be able to surrender the Henry to its owner. I had fired probably six to ten shots and could see by the movement of hats and arms and glimpses of other upper portions of bodies behind the rebel works that the new danger was making a stir among them. It was this condition of things that absorbed my attention to the point of leaning too far back to take a shot at a new point when I discovered my own peril.

The only explanation I could ever devise for my escape from the keen eyes, which could detect a finger above our headlogs, was this: My height, added to our breastworks and the headlog on which I stood, made my head appear about twelve feet up that big tree's body from the ground. So intently were the rebels, along the line to which I was exposed, watching the regimental line of fire under the headlogs that, for that moment of my exposure, not dreaming of a human head or body, at that height, they did not notice me. The exposure was very brief, but long enough to have ended me if I had not been favored by the circumstances indicated, or some others.

There was no federal line in front of us then; nor was one ever afterward built there.

I cannot now recall, if I knew, who owned that Henry rifle. I have no doubt that I did then know and my vague impression somehow is that the owner, or holder, or borrower was a Company B man.

Scattered through this record, in various places, will be found protests and explanations with reference to the false claims of the Illinois men as to positions and movements on these fateful days and reasons for them. Shortly, as stated over and over for years now, *the 52d save all that was saved at Kenesaw.* The Illinoisans have never granted it, even grudgingly, the mead [sic] of credit and praise justly due it; and I am sure now they never will do it such justice. The facts remain, however, and they shall not obscure or dim its glory in Ohio.

I am about to touch the very heart of truth in all this achievement, and if the 52d were all alive today, they would with unanimity sustain my statement of facts and the striking conclusion which flows out from them on the crest of Kenesaw.

Note: See my correspondence file—Work—Sept. 1904, for some items bearing on this matter. 9, 23, '04.[28]

Chapter One

A day came in the history of the 52d Ohio, when its 600 men fell into new drill hands and those hands were mine, almost utterly inexperienced in warfare, at that time. It was at *Brentwood, Tennessee*. I stepped from the line to the field; Rothacker stepped into the Captaincy and Miser stepped into the Lieutenancy of Company G. It was at the beginning of May 1863.[29]

It was not many days until the regiment, in the field south of the camp, felt a new sensation. Its drill had always been after the sturdy, set forms of the books of tactics, in movements and manual of arms. These it knew quite well. The sensation first came, when, the boys standing at a front, order arms, I described a new movement, one not in the books, and described it so clearly that when the orders were given, they could as clearly and as easily obey.[30] My recollection now is that we had been on the usual afternoon drill and I managed to finish up with the regiment, at the southern side of the field furthest from the camp, in line facing the pike. The gist of the instructions were that when the "shoulder arms" had been executed, I should give the order "right face," and when that had been executed, I should order "right shoulder shift," then, "arms at ease," when the files should sidestep so that when each man dropped his rifle level across his shoulders back of his neck neither butt nor muzzle of his gun should be near enough the butt or muzzle of a comrade's gun to interfere in marching with the guns in that position and spaces and distances must be carefully preserved while they marched with "arms at ease" across the field to the edge of the woods in which was our camp. The right hand of each man was to be over the point of the butt and his left hand over the muzzle.

"Shoulder arms." "Right face." "Right shoulder shift arms." "Arms at ease." "Forward march." It was a pretty spread and splendid march.

From that day, under my hand the 52d was doing new things on the drill ground whenever we were in camp; things no other regiment was doing in the way of entirely original fancy drill, running through the whole gamut, including a manual of arms. The 52d could form a cross instantly, which was a regular hedgehog against cavalry. It could order arms from a "support" or a "right shoulder shift" as easily as others could from a simple "shoulder." These are merely specimens.

The interest and the pride of men and officers in this new drill was

Movements and Positions in the Battle of Kennesaw Mountain

sincere and steadily maintained. They appreciated what it gave them, their reputation of "the best drilled regiment in the 14th Corps," and they maintained that interest and pride and reputation on down to Lee and Gordon's Mills,[31] where just before the 1st of May 1864, Dan McCook ordered out the Third Brigade and directed me to drill it in some of the new movements applicable to the brigade. Officers of the Illinois regiments were, some of them, not quite satisfied with that order, but Dan stood in the edge of the field not far from his tent and I drilled the Third Brigade in the field east of the road and north—some distance—from the mills. The movements proposed were clearly explained and the orders given easily understood, but the 52d was "out of sight" in execution and that did not decrease the under-breath swearing of some of our Illinois friends.

Some of the fancy drill, in fact most of it, for the warfare of those days was not great practical applications, or utility, on the tactical theory of the time, but note: The 52d Ohio had become like a blacksnake whip in my hand; its confidence in itself; the touch of its comrades with each other; its "rally on the flag" when all broken and mixed up; its *esprit du corps*; its hang together disposition; its unification, were, under the training given it, well-nigh perfect, when it moved out 519 strong from Lee and Gordon's Mills at the opening of May 1864, to enter on the Atlanta Campaign. I have said enough to show my point.

We entered on that long bloody campaign; we lost by battle in killed and wounded and otherwise by sick and disabled; we did no drilling, or regular camping, in more than four solid months, May, June, July, August and into September, but the discipline and the courage of the regiment knew no abatement. There were no fancy movements on those deadly fields, but the *impetus*, so to speak, the comraderie, the confidence, the touch of elbow, were in every heart, just as the drill of the A, B, C, and the Speller and the Primer and the Reader and the rudiments of education are in the possessor of highest literary attainments, well-nigh unconsciously. They were there all the same.

These are some of the things which made the regiment superior to its fellows when the supreme trial came at Kenesaw. Now, a few words as to the why and how.

The 52d was never drilled in retreat; it was never familiarized, in the

Chapter One

smallest degree, with the idea of going backward. Its men generally were of a high order of intelligence; an influential and unusual number of them were men of superior education. It had more college and university men in it than any regiment of the division, according to my careful research and inquiry and knowledge while we were in the field, and prior to Chickamauga. I have no *definite* statistics, no figures, but I remember my investigations, impressions and conclusion in the premises.

These things made the 52d what it was at Kenesaw and made it the savior of all that was saved on that field. Tenaciously, it hung together, preserved its line, kept the touch of the elbow, and, in my judgment, would, as a fighting unit, with high intelligence and perfect drill and patriotism, have gone down to death and destruction sooner than become demoralized. It was the rallying point of the broken Third Brigade and saved that day, by qualities of nerve and courage, which were never surpassed on any field.

These views have been entertained for almost forty years, now, and they may be found among the line of my private correspondence, through all that time, but their publication would scarcely be advisable. Our comrades of the Illinois and Indiana regiments of the brigade might misunderstand them and feel aggrieved at the claim in our behalf and its assertion. This should not be, but the human heart is deceitful above all things and desperately wicked and would pervert the truth and quarrel with it.

Kenesaw was saved by the drill ground of the 52d O.V.I. at Brentwood and the drill ground of the same regiment at Lee and Gordon's Mills.[32]

It was merely another illustration of the slender thread on which often hang great results.

The saying that "The Battle of Waterloo was won on the playing fields of Eton," was attributed to Wellington. Whether he was the author or not, the saying illustrates my point with reference to the 52d and Kenesaw.

Two

When the foregoing sketch of "Movements and Positions at Kenesaw" was written, at odd times, near the close of the year 1903, the purpose was that it should be my last word about that battle and should not see the light of any sort of publicity while I lived. There is but one draft of the work, in my own handwriting—no copy has ever been made of any portion of it.

There is probably a sufficient statement of my reasons for such silence in the text as written; of this, at this distance in time, I am not quite certain, and it is not material whether or not any reason is given.

In the year 1914 abundant reason, in my judgment, arose for adding a second chapter to the observations of 1903, on the subject of Kenesaw, and, accordingly, I proceed to set down in writing what the new conditions suggest to my mind. Publication is for later determination.

From the date of the organization of the brigade at Louisville, Kentucky, which embraced the 85th, 86th and 125th Illinois Volunteer infantry regiments and the 52d Ohio Volunteer Infantry, with Colonel Dan McCook of the latter regiment in command, there was a small coterie or clique of Illinois officers, gradually enlarged as time went on, that was never satisfied with McCook's designation as brigade commander.[1]

The first and main ground of discontent was of civil and political origin, so to speak, overlooking the military reasons. There were three Illinois regiments and but one Ohio regiment in the organization to begin with; it seemed to the "complainants" that this was a disregard of the majority rule; Illinois and not Ohio should have furnished the commander of a brigade composed so largely of Illinois troops. This point of complaint rankled with the members of the very small bunch of very small souls composing the discontents or malcontents.

Chapter Two

In the second place, McCook, who had some military experience in more than a year's service in the field, a part of it as a Captain on the staff of his brother Gen. Alex McCook,[2] gave those political and civilian officers offense by the application and enforcement, as he was in simple duty bound to enforce them, of rigid military rules and orders, and members of the cabal, who had the misfortune to fall into the brigade commander's chastising hands, or under his reprimanding tongue, as time went on, were not apt to have their tempers or dispositions improved by the punishments or corrections administered.

The great body of officers and men, like Col. Harmon and Col. Dilworth and Col. Irons[3] were far above any such conspiracy or want of fidelity to a faithful commander set over them by authority.

I am owner of the Brigade Book, confided to my custody, after the incoming of the twentieth century, by Col. John J. McCook of New York City, the last survivor of Col. Dan's brothers and his nephew, Hon. Geo. W. McCook, son of Col. George W. McCook, both the latter of Steubenville, Ohio, all of them now passed away.

The record runs from September 21st, 1862, to December 31, 1863. There are 115 pages and there are 722 entries. The pages are 15½ by 10 inches; cases or matters are entered and numbered on the left hand pages, while the opposite pages are devoted to remarks on the several cases or matters.

No officer of the "Third Brigade," who conducted himself properly, within that period, is mentioned in that record as an offender against military law or his duty, in any way; but the resentment and bad blood of some of the clique toward Dan McCook may find explanation in the pages of this important volume.

Before the assault was made on Kenesaw Mountain, the 22d Indiana Volunteer Infantry became connected with and thereafter remained a part of the brigade; the 110th Illinois had served a while with it and the 69th Ohio had served with it on the 18th and 19th days of September 1863, in the opening of the battle of Chickamauga.[4]

Prior to the opening of the Atlanta Campaign, the little nest of vipers had concocted a scurrilous and cowardly scandal and libel against Dan McCook and the 52d Ohio for publication in a Peoria, Illinois, newspaper, as the contribution of the "Hd Qrs Cook." It was finished and ready for the

Movements and Positions in the Battle of Kennesaw Mountain

editor and publisher at Chattanooga, Tennessee, between the dates of the battle of Chickamauga, September 19–21, 1863, and the battle of Mission Ridge, November 24–25, next ensuing, and while the Peoria man to whom it was sent was too manly, or too much of a lawyer, or both, to print and publish the vile anonymous screed, its authors issued it secretly, spreading copies clandestinely where they supposed they could hurt Dan McCook and the 52d O.V.I. by poisoning the social and military air which they breathed.[5] They sought so to plant a real Upas tree[6] in the camps of the Colonel commanding the McCook brigade of the reserve Corps—later the 3d brigade, second division, 14th Army Corps, Army of the Cumberland, and the 52d O.V.I, of which he was the ranking and commanding officer.

At the very outset, let it be repeated with strongest emphasis, that the great mass of the staff and field and line, officers and men, of the Illinois regiments named was loyal and true to each other and to their comrades of other states. Only the dirty dogs, the sneaks and snipers, the willing and cowardly assassins of character and reputation, modern Borgias, could foster and follow such spirits and ends.

It is not the purpose, because it is not necessary, to reproduce in full the work of the ugly fiends, in human forms, among their fellows.

I have a copy of that anonymous production. It opens with these descriptive words:

> Twenty-Two General Rules to Be Observed by Colonels Commanding Brigades and More Especially by Those Who Aspire to the Position of Brigadier Generals Compiled from Actual Observation at Hd Qrs of the ___ Brig ___ Div Reserve Corps
> Army of the Cumberland Col _____ Commanding
> By Hd Q'rs Cook
> Chattanooga, Tenn. 1863

There are twelve large sized letter sheets of the manuscript, in ordinary handwriting. The typewriter had not been invented, or was not in general use, in 1863.

The tirade was devoted to besmirching and discrediting Col. Dan McCook and the 52d O.V.I. without naming him or numbering the regiment.

A very few extracts will suffice to show the exact character of the whole paper.

Chapter Two

[*Rule*] 5. Be sure and have but one regiment in your Brigade from your own state, and the other three and the Battery from Illinois. By this arrangement you will be certain that your Brigade in Battle will do honor to any commander—even if the Illinois regiments have to "fix Bayonets" to keep your regiment in position. (See history of the battle of Perryville, Ky., as vouched for by many officers of the Brigade referred to.)[7]

8. Buy up a newspaper at home with the "greenbacks" your A.Q.M. and A.A.C.S. have saved while handling government stores and rations, to blow for you, and employ your chief of staff in writing puffatory notices of you to be published in those papers you can hire to print his communications. (See account of great battle between 52d O.V.I., and Wheeler's brigade of cavalry, on the Murfreesboro road, as published in the Cincinnati *Commercial* in January last, wherein it was stated that the only man engaged on the side of the union, was the redoubtable Colonel of the 52d O.V.I. against 3,000 rebel cavalry, and the loss of the enemy was reported to be "several killed," "many wounded," and a number taken prisoners, all of whom were taken off by the foolish General Wheeler!)[8]

13. When there is no danger, you had better take your escort and ride boldly forward, out of the dust, and choose a large, comfortable residence for your headquarters during the night; but if there is the smallest show of danger keep close to the Brigade. If you should overtake the rear-guard of the enemy, and a mounted "reb." should fire a shot, you should immediately fall back behind the infantry, taking your mounted escort with you at a 2–40 gait not frightened, of course! Here you can be safe, and order the infantry to pursue the mounted "rebel" (Vide Chronicles of the Blowing Springs?).[9]

14. If one of the guards discharges his gun, and runs to the main body, and informs you that "the 'rebs.' have wounded me," and shows you his shoe torn by a snag, by all means stop the march, and send a regiment back to find the rebel, with instructions that if they fail to find him, to burn the nearest town, with all the furniture and clothing possessed by the poor half-starved wretches residing in it. Or if the soldier strays from his command and shoots a pig or a chicken, and the rear-guard fails to detect him in it, you must conclude that the shots were fired by guerillas, and order the guards to fire by volley into the adjacent hills, woods and orchards, no matter if some poor contraband belonging to an officer should be murdered by this random firing. Then with lighted torches bid red glaring havoc reign around until not a tenement is left, and naught but blackened stones remain as monuments of your bravery and devotion to the Union. (See the official reports of the great battles of Lynnville and Pigeon Roost, near Pulaski.)[10]

16. If the rebels have at any time handled your brother rather severely on the high road, (while he was out of his place,) when your Brigade arrives in that neighborhood, you should detail a large party, arm them with axes, torches, and other implements of destruction, and order them to girdle all the fruit trees, destroy the crops and subsistence; pile up the fences into mighty trophies, apply the torch to the houses, barns, out-houses and cotton sheds; scare the trembling women and naked children to the woods, and the damp, dark caves for shelter,

Movements and Positions in the Battle of Kennesaw Mountain

there to perish with hunger; for having shot the cows, sheep and hogs, you have wrenched from them every hope for future subsistence. Thus you will cause your brother's spirit to rest well "in that bourne from whence no traveller returns," and will secure yourself a memorial if not a name in history. The memorial will be traced in the blood-red hand of destruction in characters that mark the place where pleasant dwellings were burned, and happy families destroyed. No fear it will last forever!

The great advantage of this kind of warfare is, that it throws great numbers of outcasts upon the charity of the Government, which may while it feeds, convert them. Or if they are left to starve, they cannot rebel against the Union.[11]

These paragraphs will suffice, as stated, to show the character and spirit of the whole diatribe and its authors.

The proper place for the authors of that production was in a rebel regiment, if they had the courage above that of a louse, and not in a fighting federal brigade. It was an error to consign them to a rebel regiment except so far as the rebel argument and sentiment were concerned, for no honorable Confederate soldier would be willing to associate with that sort of conspirator or liar.

I have no evidence—never had any—that the hounds brought it to the notice of Col. Dan or his chief of staff, then Capt. Edw. L. Anderson of Cincinnati, Ohio.

The spleen, the resentment and the malice of the gang followed the Colonel through the remainder of his life and has sought to becloud and reflect on his memory even down to this day.

I quote from one of the letters of the Third Brigade Illinois officer written September 17, 1903, some considerable time, it will be observed, after Dan McCook was beyond the reach of the writer's active ill-will or malevolent silence. He was writing to a brother Illinois officer of the same brigade. Hear him:

> They gave up all they had which was life, and he did no more; the fact that he had a commission and was in command of the Brigade placed more responsibility upon him, perhaps, than upon them, and possibly, if he had handled his men a little better, his own life as well as some of theirs might have been spared. I have no desire [of course not] to belittle the services of Col. McCook in an way and have never [hardly ever] said one word against him and never [hardly ever, again] shall [shall what?] unless I should be placed in a position where it would be necessary for me to give my recollections of what occurred there, which is not likely to happen.

Chapter Two

Some of the McCooks were then alive—the brothers are all dead now—and one of them, who listened to Confederate guns in the Western Army until the close of Chickamauga and to the same sort of music in the Army of the East down to Appomatox,[12] sent to me the letter containing this extract, and I had occasion to write to another of the McCooks on the 5th day of October, next ensuing, the following comments on the observations of the Illinois officer, aforesaid:

> The paragraph is *Illinois* from beginning to end. It is the one next the last, beginning, "I have no personal interest" and ending "not likely to happen." It is written evidence of the cowardly meanness, which pervaded the breasts of the clique while in the field. I have on my files a shameful measure of that spirit, which, perhaps, never came to the knowledge of the Colonel or yourself and it will be just as well that you do not learn it, if there is the faintest hope of a satisfactory Kenesaw monument.
> The sneaking, insidious, egotistical suggestion of the author in the words, "and, possibly, if he had handled his men a little better his own life as well as some of theirs might have been spared," is only equaled by the arrant hypocrisy and dirty spirit in the remaining words of the paragraph, to wit: "I have no desire to belittle the services of Co. McCook in any way [of course not] and have never said one word against him and never shall [never shall what?] unless I should be placed in a position where it would be necessary for me to give my recollections of what occurred there, which is not likely to happen."
> You were not in position, for several reasons, to comment on this sort of stuff; I am at such liberty, at least, confidentially, to you. I pass the bad grammar and bad rhetoric, without comment. The understanding is that this fellow is a lawyer and that he has made, or inherited, or married, some money, possibly all three. He knows enough law to veil a libel and plainly has common sense enough to understand a libelous hint to the groundlings while he pretends to the charity of silence about the "dreadful things" locked up with the secrets of his breast.
> Captain C, come out with your secrets.[13] The call should be made on him to tell all he knows about Dan. McCook at the "dead angle. It is necessary now for him to give those recollections, while there are men still living who can give them the lie successfully, if they discount, in the smallest degree, the courage or capacity or conduct of Dan McCook at Kenesaw. It is in the fortieth year since the object of this insidious attack went down to his death and in that forty years no man, to my knowledge has ever before this breathed a syllable, openly or covertly, reflecting, in any way, upon the Kenesaw memory of the gallant leader of the Third Brigade, or his action there. It is rather late for this malignant to tell a story of misconduct against him which will stand for a moment before the truth. Come out in the open, you prima facie libeler of the dead. The necessity, behind the alleged absence of which you seek to hide, is on you now to give the survivors of the

Movements and Positions in the Battle of Kennesaw Mountain

Third Brigade those "recollections" for analysis, comparison and refutation. The necessity to speak has happened.

Dan McCook was not without his faults and infirmities—none of us is—but they did not empeach his military conduct or record and the spirit that would stab even an enemy in the back, or libel the memory of the dead, directly or by indirection, had no place in his make-up or nature. He was too bluffly honest and outspoken for such insincerity.

When Mr. C—— wrote that letter, he placed himself in a "position" where it was "necessary" for him to "give" those "recollections." The fellow overreached himself and ought to be driven to the wall—compelled to speak and vindicate his aspersions or take his punishment for the vile insinuation, "which lacks the essential element of truth," that, if he must speak, he will discredit Dan McCook.

The latter must have been nearly in the right place if he was keeping "within ten feet" of Captain C——; so Davis' position cannot consistently be criticized by the Captain. If the latter gave the Colonel some order or supposed nugget of military wisdom, which the Colonel then disregarded, his conduct might be defended, if we knew what the Captain did or said, in that respect. If the latter saw something omitted, which Dan ought to have done, and did not speak to Dan about it, "possibly" the Captain, if anybody, was in fault.

By all means, having said so much, he ought to be given the witness stand and compelled to speak his *suppressed recollections*. If he and the Colonel were not alone in the assault, at that point, there may be others, who have "recollections." Let him say, if he will, that they were alone. I have said too much on the subject, perhaps, but the ugly spirit and shallow cunning make me "warm under the collar"; I despise a skulker, a character or reputation assassin, who discloses his own malice and cowardice in the effort to stab his victim, dead or alive, under cover, equivalent to false pretenses, in secret or in the grave.

With my wife as a travelling companion, I spent the time from May 13th to May 27, 1897, both inclusive, visiting camps and battlefields with which I had some personal familiarity during the Civil War, from the Ohio River at Cincinnati and Louisville to Jonesboro, Georgia, twenty miles below Atlanta.[14]

On that excursion, going south, we visited, May 21st and 22d, Marietta and the Kenesaw battle grounds. I had passed through there with the 52d by rail from Atlanta to northern Alabama, September 30th, 1864, and on the march going south again, November 14th, next following, and these had been my only views, before this visit, after we left the breastworks on Kenesaw on the morning of July 3d, 1864.

One outcome of this southern trip is described in a letter to my

Chapter Two

brother A.R., then of Cincinnati, who was with me in the 52d. He died April 19, 1913.

Columbus, O., Dec. 25, 1902.

Dear Brother:
Yours from Cincinnati yesterday will be very freely answered—how fully, I'll not now say, because I do not know—but all I may say on each of your two principal subjects will be *in the strictest confidence*. The reasons in the second matter you already fully understand; those in the first I hope to make appear.
Kenesaw.
Lucy and I visited our camps and battlefields from the Ohio river to Jonesboro, Georgia, in May 1897, immediately after the first wedding in our house. On that visit, I met, and reviewed Kenesaw in company with, the owner of the farm on which the latter half of the charge was made and the works of the confederates assaulted and—at the close of the charge—the works of McCook's and Mitchell's brigades were constructed.

The lines were there distinctly, but husbandry was gradually destroying some of the features of the landscape. Thirty three years had gone by and no one had moved in the *direction of preservation and protection* of the famous field.

Upon our return from the south, I opend a correspondence with the owner of Kenesaw, which resulted in my purchase of his farm—sixty five acres—in 1898. The contract of purchase was signed and delivered; maps, plate and abstracts were made and delivered to me and my three years lease back to the former owner was written, signed and in his hands; my check was ready for delivery and the deed to me was due, when the owner showed some signs of wishing to *retain his land*, of rueing his sale. I had my plans and purposes for the future of the land laid out, in a general way, and had given a good deal of time to the negotiations and the purchase, the owner being a sort of stupid and slow of comprehension, but the land was the man's home and as I had not an atom of selfishness, or self-serving, in the matter, I did not wish to have the uncomfortable feeling that the lifetime owner would always feel regret that he had parted with the title. Out of this—I may call it—generous feeling, on my part, and not otherwise, I permitted him to cancel the contract of sale and return it and [the] lease to myself.

I have in my possession every word and scrap of correspondence and documents, with, and from everybody, in the premises, but I have not reviewed them since each went on my files, in the usual course of business. These facts are mentioned for two reasons;

1. What I say is backed by black and white, by day and date;
2. I do not, without examination, attempt to state the latter—days and dates— without absolute accuracy.

About this time the contract of purchase was signed and delivered I advised "a

Movements and Positions in the Battle of Kennesaw Mountain

52d officer of Cincinnati" of the fact of the purchase. Immediately, he assumed that I would transfer the property to the general government and asked me by letter to use my influence to have him appointed a park commissioner of Kenesaw.

As I recall the correspondence with him, I did not jump with the conclusion that I had bought Kenesaw for the general government, though it might later on seem best to make such a transfer.

I disclosed to no other man on earth the fact of my purchase until after the cancellation; kept it for the time even from my wife.

I think my contract price was $1,350; the instrument expressed the sum.

About the time of the cancellation, I received a letter from an Illinois officer of the brigade written at Chicago and two letters from another written at Peoria, or in the vicinity, about buying the Kenesaw land. They did not hint that they knew of my purchase; they wrote as though they were originators of the plan to purchase and wished to enlist me in the enterprise as a 52d officer. The letters struck me as peculiar productions, on a peculiar subject, in view of my negotiations with the owner, and coming at a peculiar time and while not arousing any marked suspicion in my mind at the moment, they "left a queer taste in my mouth."

[I answered the first from Peoria, but neither of the others, for the lapse of a little time persuaded me that certain Illinois gentlemen had somehow induced the owner to renig on his sale to me *so that they might acquire title to Kenesaw.*]

They bought the land for $1000.

Gradually, it dawned upon me that through fear of the glorification of the 52d, if I became the absolute owner of the field, and through fear of my private ownership, and control, some of the officers had, by trick, or fraud, or lies—I don't know exactly how—broken my contract for Kenesaw for their own supposed advantage. It was an unmanly and unsoldierly way to treat me. No one, as I say, had ever moved in the business until I did in 1897–1898, and when I had done so, instead of coming out in the open with me to have the Brigade buy and dispose of the land and making such a proposal to me as the man, who was equitable owner, with power to enforce the conveyance of the legal title to himself, they played a successful sneak. Of course, if I had suspected such a meanness it never would have succeeded, though I was indifferent as to who might own and care for the land, i.e, as I have said, in effect, I had no personal or even regimental ambition in buying it.

As soon as it became perfectly clear to my mind that the scurvy trick had been practiced and my conjectures of reasons for it assumed fairly definite features, I said to myself, "*God prosper the care of Kenesaw, but I'll never make a move nor do a thing, in that business, which any man, or officer, or set of men, large or small, can, in their sleeves, or behind their beer glasses, tip off as 'dancing at my own funeral.'*"

From that day to this I have had neither art nor part nor lot in the matter, or the controversies which may have arisen in brigade business, and, as I see it, I shall go on my own quiet way to the end, without mixing in the differences or being identified with Kenesaw *business*, in the slightest degree. There is now a

Chapter Two

tangle among the brethren about charters and powers and policies. They can fight them out "for all me"—I am not in the fights, though I might if I wished [to] join those who are opposing the party led by the tricksters.

One of the two holders to the legal title to the land, who says they are "trustees," submitted to me a simple legal question about the trust last week. Disclaiming all interest in any controversy, in the premises, I gave him a legal opinion, on general principles, founded on the few facts and the legal conclusion which he stated to me, and then told him he ought to describe the *trust* and all its terms and conditions, which he had not given me, to some good Illinois lawyer and be guided by him in the execution of such trust.

I think I know the names of some of the Illinois gentlemen whose fine Italian hands were at work with my business, unsuspected, and who succeeded in *pie*-ing it. I have no resentment toward them, though I love a manly man and despise the indirection of a fellow, who cannot look me squarely in the face, because he has injured, or tried to injure, me or some of my friends.

I may be liable to be misunderstood in holding absolutely aloof from the business of the Third Brigade so far as it affects Kenesaw. Be it so. I have the *mens conscia recti*[15] and so, at this late day in life, reck little what the mongers may say. Not likening myself to Him, but, as the striking illustration of the ages, I remember the Saviour of mankind was crucified between two thieves, Himself not only innocent, but a benefactor.

Now, I think you will grasp that situation. I have another point, which is, at present, a mere query, to suggest.

As your letter shows, and as I understand, there is a difference in the brigade on the subject of title and control of Kenesaw, i.e, one faction is in favor of governmental ownership and control, while another faction is in favor of brigade ownership and control through corporate action by 'trustees' of the land.

Into the merits of that controversy I enter not.

When the Cincinnati officer went from Kenesaw in September last to Asheville, N.C., where he still is, he wrote me a long letter, which argued for governmental control, the same view to which he "jumped" when I confided to him my purchase of the property in 1898. He showed me quite fully the history of some phases of the troubles about the land and its control. I did not find time to hurry my answer. Presently another wrote me some account of the Kenesaw reunion and touched on the differences that were brewing about the characters and title and control. I wrote both that I could have no part in them, but out of it all a strange thought, for the first time, flashed into my mind. As I said above, it is a query: Did the Cincinnati officer, when I confided to him my purchase of Kenesaw, betray it to the Illinois men at Peoria and aid, or join, them in breaking my contract through the feat that I would not convey to government and he might not become a government commissioner?

I am slow to assent, but, the facts and the dates, as my memory now recalls them, *fit* the affirmative precisely; the coincidences, to say the least, are remarkable.

Movements and Positions in the Battle of Kennesaw Mountain

He was the only human being in Ohio, except myself, who knew it, or who could tell it.

The Illinois letters referred to were queer in the ways I have pointed out, and they came *after* I confided to the Cincinnati officer.

The letters of the owner toward the last were not quite clear and needed explanation.

Now, the planning and scheming are, apparently, obvious.

But I neither accuse the Cincinnati officer nor find him guilty now. I shall be shocked if ever forced to the conclusion of his guilt by the facts. *If* he did the thing, which I suggest as a possibility, it was basest treason to friend and friendship and social confidence.

I then had no suspicion, until say the date of, or immediately after, the cancellation. If I am spared until I can find the time to go into my library and take down and read the entire correspondence, with the owner, with the Cincinnati officer, with the Illinois officers, covering the transactions mentioned, in the order of time, with comparison of dates and developments of propositions, plans and ideas, I expect the perusal to work a firm moral conviction, one way or the other, in the premises. I shall see behind precise and comparative dates and expressions, I think, what I did not dream of as events took place until about the climax and with which I did not, in any form or manner, connect the Cincinnati officer until the month of November 1902.

I now know the Cincinnati officer to be in close touch with, at least, one of the Illinois officers, who wrote me in the strange way, at the strange juncture of time and events. I'll wait. You remember Horace, somewhere, says justice is slow of foot, but in the end knocks at every door. The thing will come out in the end.

Thus, at some length, though not in the detail which might add to its clearness, I have given you my relation to Kenesaw. Enclosed I hand you copy of my last letter to the Cincinnati officer, to which he has not yet responded.

I shall attempt to influence no man in the Kenesaw business, but I have stepped aside from the imbroglio of its authors and, for the reasons suggested, like Tom Corwin, when he separated in principle from his political party, at one time, "I am in a crowd by myself."[16] That resolution was taken not only for the then present, but for all the future.

Down to this point in my writing of this letter, I purposely refrained from reading the Cincinnati officer's letter to you, proceeding simply on the suggestions of your letter and the "facts of the case" from my standpoint. His letter is herewith returned. I have read it. The Illinois officer is the 86th officer who has been active,[17] and he and the Cincinnati officer have been *cooperative*. You can, from the letter to you, see the umbilical cord between them. The Illinois officer was one of the men who wrote to me at the *opportune* (?) time.

The trustee—McGinness[18] of Peoria—who submitted the legal question to me stated that the first corporation chartered which I think they call K.M.A.[19] has no power under its charger to take, or hold, or control title to land; that a second corporation—I don't remember its name, if he stated it—has such power under its

Chapter Two

charter. Both these corporations are organized within the brigade, under Illinois law, and, in some way, they represent the conflicting views and policies of members of the brigade association.

It would be the last thing above ground that I would do, to wit: to take a hand in what the Cincinnati officer styles "this muddle," and then I would not do it; 1st, on general principles and, 2dly, for the special reasons suggested in this letter.

The Cincinnati officer is making interest with you for the climax of the contest, which seems to be on and with which I shall not be concerned, thank the good Lord.

There comes to my mind, just now, the contents of a letter written by an 86th officer not long ago, which showed profound distrust and jealousy of the 52d and the imputation of selfish, vain-glorious and overreaching motives and purposes on the part of Col. John J. McCook and myself in connection with the Kenesaw business. I have defined myself. I have not communicated, directly or indirectly, with John McCook in thirty seven years. The letter was a confidential communication and the author, whom I know, never expected it to fall, even temporarily, into my hands. As touching myself and the regiment, I know, and as touching McCook, I believe, it was a tissue of falsehoods, pure inventions, from first to last; I made, could make, no response to it. It was merely amusing to read the play of imagination and unpatentable invention without any feeling of either right or obligation to call the author down hard.

I don't care a *sou marque*[20] about who wins; I do not expect ever in this life to see the ground again though I hope to go down the R.R. past it once more in the uncertain future. It was, in my judgment, the greatest little battle of the war, intense, compressed, unique, and it ought to be fittingly commemorated by monuments and markers on the ground; but I have "stepped aside," except as to its glory and its history, a rather full record of which my children will find in my writings, if they care to stop long enough to turn over the printed and written pages.

And now, to state the chief proposition which has called forth this chapter on Kenesaw:

Illinois has planted her Illinois monument on ground captured and held by Ohio solders June 27—July 2, 1864, and of which no Illinois troops were ever in possession, for one moment, within that period.[21]

The State of Illinois had no purpose to cast a reflection of any sort on the State of Ohio by that act; the State of Illinois was kept in ignorance of the exact facts or it would not have loaned itself to the scheme of those who have used it to erect on Kenesaw a monument to Illinois troops on ground which belongs peculiarly and exclusively for such a purpose to Ohio troops.

Ohio has no objection to an Illinois monument to Kenesaw Mountain

Movements and Positions in the Battle of Kennesaw Mountain

in celebration of the part taken by Illinois troops in the assault of June 27, 1864, not the slightest; it could have none. Ohio has no criticism of the character of the structure erected there and dedicated on the 27th day of June 1914, but Ohio does object to the appropriation by Illinois of ground which Illinois troops never passed or fought over and never, for an instant, held or occupied, and which Ohio troops both charged and fought over and held, exclusively.

This appropriation was deliberately and knowingly, with malice prepense, planned and perpetrated by the surviving spirits of the clique of 1863.

They know that they have devised and executed a supplanting act; that they have taken ground and sought to take credit on Kenesaw which never belonged to Illinois troops and which peculiarly and specially belonged to the 52d Ohio Volunteer Infantry.

The achievement of the Ohio regiment in that assault was distinguished, marked and unique, unapproached and unequalled by any achievement of any other state troops on that field; indeed, a marshalling and contrast of the conduct of Ohio and Illinois officers and men there left and leaves Illinois doing all that any soldier or historian could expect or require at their hands in the way of dash or bravery and sacrifice, but the truth gives to the 52d Ohio a thing done on Kenesaw which outshines them all and which alone saved the day and the glory—all there was of it—on that mountain-side. If the 52d had not hung together and shown a steadiness and pluck and drill and endurance unsurpassed in the supreme crisis of the battle, Illinois would have shared the same fate and followed the same defeated course as Harker's brigade and been driven from the field.[22]

Illinois solders and historians have from thence hitherto carefully abstained from any mention of the special work and its results of the 52d Ohio, at that crucial point, in that assault. They never refer to the solemn fact, solemn for them—they may think the argument from its [sic] makes it an ugly fact—that, while the 52d Ohio started from the ridge in the rear—the fifth regiment—of the brigade column, when it lay down, at the rebel breastworks, within fifty to seventy feet of the muzzles of blazing, smoking rebel rifles, the Illinois troops, which had started in front of it had been driven before those rifles like chaff before a storm down that

Chapter Two

mountain side into flight and disorganization, seeking safety from the visitation of a burning hell, and the Illinois regiments were all scattered down the slope and across the little meadow or wheat-field behind it.

If any Illinois writer or orator has ever recited or referred to this fact in the last fifty one years, the reference has been so infrequent and obscure as wholly to escape observation.

It has been more comfortable to slur over or pervert these facts, or to maintain entire silence about them and refer to the "bear which me and the old woman killed," divide credit and glory with the 52d in "glittering generalities," and then as far as possible ignore the Ohio regiment.

Recalling the spirits in the nasty "screed" of 1863, a 52d Ohio boy in retaliation might, at this exact point in the sketch of Kenesaw, ask the survivors of the clique what their "screed" theory had to do with placing the 52d in rear of the brigade for the assault on Kenesaw and what in practice when it was left alone under those guns an hour later at the dead angle on June 27, 1864?

It is "[Rule] 5" and it will do to quote it again by way of refreshment.

> [Rule] 5. Be sure and have but one regiment in your Brigade from your own state, and the other three and the Battery from Illinois. By this arrangement you will be certain that your Brigade in Battle will do honor to any commander—even if the Illinois regiments have to "fix Bayonets" to keep your regiment in position. (See history of the battle of Perryville, Ky., as fouched for by many officers of the Brigade referred to.)

Dreadful as the slaughter was, that 52d boy, who knew the "screed" and the history of the clique, as he lay up next to the rebel breastworks in front of all of Illinois' fighting men, who had rushed to the rear pell mell at that hour and were scattered to the rear, as already shown, might have been pardoned if, on looking around, he had chuckled to himself and asked "where are the Perryville bayonets? and what has become of last year's dirty libelers, the screed writers?"

It is dead sure that they were not all killed at Kenesaw, or anywhere else on the tramp, or in battle, as far as Durham Station, North Carolina.

In the light of, and not to repeat, the statements of "Movements and Positions at Kenesaw,"[23] let us look closely at some things never dwelt on, but gently slurred or silenced over by the schemers of this band of perverts.

Movements and Positions in the Battle of Kennesaw Mountain

The retreat of the Illinois regiments at Kenesaw began in a way just after the 52d passed the rifle pits, going up, in the edge of the woods, at the edge of the little field described. Men were breaking to the rear from the front regiments of the brigade and coming at a double quick down the hill past the right of the regiments before the 52d entered the woods, when it was about halfway from the line of the broken tree or stump, where we lay down in the little meadow, to the edge of the woods.

In the passage over this space and before we were up to the rifle pits, the rustle of men turning back, and a few of them trying to crowd through our ranks, was pronounced—so much so that Joseph K. Welt, a private of Company E, 52d O.V.I., looking up the slope and at the falling men, the wounded turning back and the whole vivid moving picture before him must have concluded that everything was on the eve of a break-up and a flight to the rear. I knew Joseph well. He faced about and took one step. Like Arnold Winkelried, the "very thought came o'er his face"[24] and being almost beside him on his left as he faced the front, I swung my outstretched arm and sword up past his person, close by his eyes, with the words, "stop, Joe!" He obeyed instantly, turned back into his place and never made a misstep afterward to my knowledge, and was in place in his company always, even down to his muster out at at Washington City, June 3, 1865, and later at Columbus, Ohio, as faithful a soldier as ever fired a rifle or fixed a bayonet.

It was at the Cadiz fair in Eastern Ohio in the fall of 1869 that I met him and for the first time mentioned the Kenesaw incident to him or any other. He had no recollection of it, or any part of it; was genuinely surprised to learn that he had faced to the rear at any time during the charge.

The first man of the 52d that I saw fall was Isaac Newton Wycoff, a corporal of Company G, whom I had enlisted and taken into the service; he had been one of my best students at Richmond College before the outbreak of the war.[25] He pitched forward as he passed the rifle pits of the enemy—not killed, but mortally wounded. Some other or others of the regiment may have fallen before him; he was the first 52d man I saw go down.

The slope up which we climbed was perhaps thirty degrees, a rather open timbered tract with considerable undergrowth obstructing our view

Chapter Two

and screening the Confederate works. It is a gravelly, clayey soil, and oak timber country, with other varieties of timber interspersed.

The noise and confusion of battle began when we started from the ridge about six hundred yards away and increased as we approached nearer and nearer the enemy's line of breastworks, changing from the roar of artillery on both sides until the rattle of musketry drowned all other sounds. We did no firing as we double-quicked down through the open field, across the little meadow or climbed the slope to the rebel works. It was not practicable for us to use rifles in the close formation of the brigade [in] active movement against the enemy's line of entrenchments.

There was no double-quicking after we rose to our feet in the little meadow; the pace was then a quick-step. As we pushed up the slope we saw and felt more and more the pressure and rush of men from the brigade to the rear. They came against and past our right wing and gradually the stream increased in numbers and strength until it bent back and the three right companies, A, F and D of the 52d and the right of Company I, but did not otherwise break their formation. The 52d held its steady upward pace. The rush and retreat of the other regiments of the brigade to get away from the deadly fire of the fortified and concealed Confederates carried them—those that were not killed or mortally wounded—past the right of the 52d in the manner described and down the slope to the rear. In the retreating crowd were wounded men and well men. There was no organization among them, of brigade or regiment or company; it had been broken. At its climax, when the 52d passed the crest, which is there yet, one hundred feet from that line of rebel breastworks, a veritable hell on earth, it had no Federal line in front of it; every regiment of the brigade which had started on the charge in front of it had been swept away, broken and demoralized by the guns of the enemy.

The hillside was strewn with the dead and wounded of all the regiments. A man who could get away, when he was hurt, did so in the speediest possible manner from running with all his remaining strength to crawling along the ground by inches, sometimes aided by a chum or comrade.

As soon as the last of the retreating mass had passed, the companies of the 52d which had been bent or broken to the rear by their defeated and retreating comrades, came forward into line and under the fearful

Movements and Positions in the Battle of Kennesaw Mountain

fire passed over the practically level ground from the crest to the rebel line and lay down in line at fifty to seventy feet from the Confederate works. When the 52d ranks sank down, its alignment faced the "dead angle," as it was afterward called, the right wing of the regiment a very little further from the earthworks of the enemy than the left by reason of the refusal of the Confederate line, which turned back at the obtuse angle and went off down the hill in the direction of Carter's eight gun battery, which, on our right, had played on the three brigades, Mitchell's, McCook's and Harker's during the charge and on the two former afterward, during the siege.

The Lieut. Col. was in command of the 52d at the right of the regiment until we reached the crest; my special charge was the left wing of the regiment and my general position in and along with the middle of that wing.[26] H was the left color company and when we were at the point of the Joe K. Welt episode, I was between the middle and the left of Company E and in going up the slope had passed along the line to the left until when the line sank down above the crest, I was with the men of Company G, close to its Captain, Samuel Rothacker, who was in his place at the head of his company, of which I had been the original Captain. It was in the line of my duty and without special thought, except as a commanding officer, exercising supervision, that I was the last man of the line to take to the earth. We were in front; there were no troops between the line of the 52d Ohio Volunteer Infantry and the cracking guns of the Confederate soldiers, whom we could not see for their earthworks, headlogs and the smoke of battle. It was the din and roar and death and wounds of the supreme exertion of human power. The cries and moans of the wounded and dying were unheard. To the unaccustomed it would seem strange that men make so little noise on such occasions. For the most part, they suffer or suffer and die quietly, a low moan, in most cases being the limit. Lying close under the guns of the Confederates, such as it was, the rebels overshot us largely, but it was possible for them in many instances, to depress their guns, as they did, under the headlogs and wound and kill men in our line, while we were so hugging the earth and within a few feet of them. This picture was painted of the hour about which I am now writing while we were still in sight of Kenesaw, but after the Confederates had abandoned that as a line of defense. Though more than fifty years have

Chapter Two

passed, the painting is like the reality and the memory is as vivid as life itself.

The letter was written to my parents at the first leisure moment after the assault and while the top of Kenesaw Mountain was still within the horizon of our camp ground or fighting line. The writing is practically contemporaneous history. I am indebted to the care of my father, who, of his own notion, preserved the letter, with others of the memorable years, and presented them all to me not long before his death in 1891.[27] The extracts are quoted literally, the one now specially reffered to is as follows:

> Here we lay until 8:30 o'clock on the morning of the 27th, a day to be remembered while time shall last.
> At the hour named, we marched along a ridge through woods until we reached an open field. Here balls from the rebel skirmish line began to disable men in the brigade. We had all learned just before moving into the open field what was to be attempted.
> The works of the enemy were to be stormed upon a wooded hill opposite the point where our brigade was formed, five regiments deep.
> Through the leaves along the crest at less than one-half mile from us, across two open fields, the works of the enemy could be partially seen. There was an ominous stillness in the ranks. All knew that many must fall and each heart communed with itself in the few brief moments of rest.... The mother, the wife, the lover, brothers and sisters doubtless occupied the thoughts of many of those brave boys. Some were gazing upon a sun that would only shine in after days to light their graves.... Others were feeling themselves perfect men for the last time. Their perfections were soon to be marred.
> Here and there was a talkative, restless, profane old soldier. I remember one who had fought at Pea Ridge and many times and places since. Said he, in my hearing, to a comrade: "Aye! God, Jim, that hill's going to be worse'n Pea Ridge. We'll ketch hell over'n them woods." This was uttered in a low tone with mysterious nods toward the opposite ridge.
> Our artillery kept pouring its iron messengers upon the devoted spot selected for our assault. The troops on our right and left were ready; on our left a salvo from a six-gun battery told that the instant had come. Away, down the long slope, across the wide bottom, the long lines of devoted men moved with a shout into the face of the foe. When we began to ascend to the works in the edge of the woods the halt and lie down were ordered, by whom I do not know.
> A perfect sheet of lead swept just over us; wounded and bloody men from what were then the front regiments began to pour back past us. "Forward," came the order and at the same instant. The line of every regiment in front of us was broken. Men came rushing down the slope in crowds breathing hard through fear and physical exhaustion.

Movements and Positions in the Battle of Kennesaw Mountain

The tide of retreat swelled until I thought at one moment my part of the regiment, the left wing, would be swept away by the throng.

Be it ever spoken to the praise of the 52d O.V.I., in that trying moment, it did not falter or waver and moved steadily on the charge with its line complete until it passed every regiment of the brigade and was halted within twenty-five yards, full view, of the rebel breastworks.

Colonel McCook had fallen. Colonel Harmon, next in command, had been shot down; the brigade had given away, as I have said, and if the truth were told and full justice done, the 52d saved all that was saved by its nerve and courage for twenty-five minutes, but in less than that time eighty-five officers and men bit the dust from our ranks.

Men gave up their lives everywhere, it seemed. You could not say or think who would die or be maimed the next instant. I shall never forget the thud of the minie ball through human flesh; it is a sickening sound, but the saddest sight I saw on that day was each time a poor fellow, near me, would be wounded and start back to the rear only to fall pierced by a death shot after he had ceased fighting. I saw in those few moments several such cases and when you know how eager the wounded man is to get off the field without being killed, you can appreciate in a degree what my feelings were. He is not afraid to die, but after being disabled in the fight he wants to live that if he must be killed it may be while he himself is able to strike blows as well as receive them.

The other regiments of the brigade were rallied and as the firing slacked up, the assault having failed, orders were issued to fortify the ground, and, until the rebels left July 2d, it was a constant fight. Night and day the deadly rifle was doing its work. Our boys shot their head logs and *chevaux de frise* to splinters killing and wounding from twenty-five to fifty of them each day, excepting the 29th of June when a truce prevailed to allow the dead lying between the works to be carried off or buried. On that day, Union and Rebel met between the works, shook hands and drank and talked as though they never had tried to kill each other.

If we had carried their works at that point, it would have been good-by to much of Hood's or *then Johnson's* [sic] *Army*. We would have been right in rear of Kenesaw. The point of assault was the *key* to the mountain, but human flesh could not do more than we did and a failure was the result. On the 2d day of July they gave my old orderly sergeant, but then Lieutenant Miser, a mortal wound. He was too brave—carelessness and a reckless despite of their attempt to kill him made him, without bravado, expose his person above our works and his life paid the forfeit.

On the 3d of July we moved from our works where a hovering death had kept our heads for the most part well ducked own and our bodies behind earthworks constantly.

Passing by the suburbs of the neat town of Marietta, some six miles south we discovered our friends again intrenched in front of us. We took matters coolly, stopping and fortifying not far from them and, during the 4th of July, shelling their pickets with twelve pounders!

Chapter Two

From the moment the 52d line sank down the men began firing at the space between the headlogs and the earth of the breastworks, which they topped. That space was approximately two or three inches, just sufficient to allow the guns to be poked through and sighted and fired. The logs were from seven to ten inches in diameter, large enough to screen and protect the head of a man as he worked his gun through such two or three inch crack. It was to leave as small a portion as possible, consistent with the use of the head and arms, of the soldier, exposed to an enemy's fire. It was against such a narrow line of opportunity as this that our men began firing. Of course they could not see a foe, but knew where that foe was and began "plugging away" at the only vulnerable line in sight, darkened, as it was, by the smoke of battle. Our fire, under the conditions, could not have been very effective, but it was not wholly lost on the men behind the fortified line, for it had a distinct influence on checking and keeping down, to some extent, the rebel fire.

The Lieut. Col. in the charge and in the mix-up that occurred by the bending or forcing back of the right companies of the regiment mentioned, after we passed the crest was separated from the line of the regiment and lost for a time and I was in sole command of it from, say, 9:20 a.m. until 4 p.m. of the 27th.

Within a half hour of the sinking down to the ground at that distance of fifty to seventy feet from the Confederate works, the little crest thirty or more feet behind us was discovered and the 52d was instructed to crawfish back to its protection. On the practically level ground between the crest and the works we were at the mercy of our adversaries and with time and patience they could have picked us all off, then to one, as in a slaughter house, but with the protection of that crest our chances of life were vastly increased. The character or nature of the brigade—a very few—were lodged so near the line of the rebel breastworks that they were, that day or night, called in over that line and made prisoners, but I never had knowledge of a 52d man who accepted such an invitation.

While the 52d clung to that hillside under favor of the slight crest, one hundred feet from the rebel line and kept up the desultory fire at the rebel headlogs, it still held the front line of the brigade, and this line, at the crest, it held until about the noon hour, while officers and men of the brigade and the other regiments were pulling themselves together, taking

Movements and Positions in the Battle of Kennesaw Mountain

stock of a disaster, and finding, in the dreadful slaughter and repulse, just where they were "at." It could not be done in a minute, in so large an affair.

As we went up the slope on the charge, the other regiments of the brigade came down the slope and bent back the right wing of the 52d, as already described. The remainder of the regiment, Companies C, H, E, K, G and B, were not disturbed in alignment, in any respect, except by the comrades who fell, dead or wounded, before the guns of the fortified enemy. The gaps so made were steadily closed up and the regimental line was disturbed and maintained as has been described, and not otherwise.

The left company of the regiment—Company B—passed just to the left of a large tree, which later stood in the line of our breastworks; none of the other regiments of the brigade passed so near that tree; their "rush to the rear" had been from a central line ascending, which was thrown to the right of the central line on which the 52d moved after we entered the woods, in the ascent of the slope, and the rush of the retreating men of the other regiments had a tendency to change, did change, the direction of the 52d to the left. Now, I repeat, the left of the 52d, going up and beyond the crest, passed to the left and clear of the big tree.

No other regiment of the brigade passed so near that tree by several feet, as did the 52d.

The swerving to the right of the other regiments as they went up through the woods and the swerving or forcing to the left of the 52d were distinctly marked by men in the 52d, the rear line of the brigade, as they looked against the face of the hill and the backs of the charging regiments and noted their own direction and movement.

In the repulse and retreat of the other regiments is found demonstrative evidence of what I am explaining. Six companies of the 52d Ohio, going up the slope, were wholly undisturbed except by having men shot out of the line and closing up the gaps so made. There was no halt, no misstep by the unhurt men in the line of the six companies. The three right companies and a part of the fourth—Company I—were broken to the rear by the mass and surge of the other retreating regiments of the brigade. By the time the line of the six and a half companies had reached what was afterward found to be the line of the crest, the retreating men had passed to the rear and, as above indicated, the right companies came forward into line and the 52d, as though on the drill field at Brentwood

Chapter Two

or at Lee and Gordon's Mills, in regimental line moved the distance of from thirty to fifty feet when, without an order, for none was needed, it went to earth, as above described.

That backward rush had not touched our left companies, because Illinois regiments were going up the slope on a line to the left or east of the line of the 52d charge, at that place, and in getting the rear after their repulse, never touched those left companies mentioned and so never touched the ground near the big tree which made an immovable landmark on Kenesaw. The tree has rotted and gone, but the tunnel mouth has been preserved and relations and distances have not changed, or been changed, in the half century and more, since these things "happened."[28]

This image shows the relative positions of the Illinois monument and the opening of the Federal tunnel that Holmes described in his memoir. The tunnel entrance, at the lower left, has now been reinforced by a small rock wall and surrounding arch (Mark A. Smith).

Movements and Positions in the Battle of Kennesaw Mountain

Was the 52d Ohio placed behind the Illinois regiments to hold the Illinois boys to their duty in the charge about to be made? Out upon the damnable thought. It never entered the brain of a 52d boy or the brain of the 85th or 86th or 125th boy, except always the members of the Illinois clique, who deserved to be cashiered and drummed out of camp; and it would have been safe to leave the punishment of that little gang of human serpents to the three Illinois regiments. The only danger in such a reference would have been in the excess of the penalty which those regiments, or a court selected from them, would have inflicted on the offenders.

It was while we lay at the crest, after the craw-fishing, as I recall it, that Captain Edward L. Anderson, of Cincinnati, chief of our Brigade staff, too sick and weak to make the charge on foot with the column, having crawled out of the bed that morning, managed to drag himself down the hill and across the little meadow and up the slope after us, as we charged, when he first came to a line of troops facing the Confederate works found himself among the men of Company K, 52 O.V.I. lying at the crest, in the position to which they had craw-fished, firing at the rebel breastworks. Captain Anderson was the Captain of Company K, 52d O.V.I., though too ill and weak to make the charge at the double-quick down that hill, across that meadow and up that slope, with the brigade column, in the line of his duty as chief of staff, he saw it start, knew its order of regiments and followed at his best speed. His own words are: *"Sick and weak I started with them and when I reached the front I was among my own men."*

The order in which he found his own brigade was simple disorder, unrecognizable until he brought up in the line of his own company, the front line of the brigade. He soon learned that McCook had been severely wounded, that Harmon had been killed and that Col. Dilworth of the 85th was in command of the brigade.

It was his duty and, under Dilworth's direction, he made the report back on the ridge to General Thomas: "I went back and reported to General Thomas, who laughingly doubted my statement regarding the position of the 52 held to the works."

General Thomas had seen the troops start on the charge; he had seen the order of the regiments in the Third Brigade; he knew that the 52d Ohio was the rear regiment of that column and, at first blush, he thought the Captain must be confused in his report of the position of that regiment

Chapter Two

in relation to the rebel works, and so far was the report out of line with his expectations and the probabilities that the General "laughingly doubted" the Captain's statement, but it was like Holy Writ.

It was out of this incident, manifestly, that the apocryphal story about Davis and Clancy grew, for upon analysis by various tests and processes, we saw in 1903, in Chapter One, how not only improbable, but how impossible was that story.[29]

This statement of the chief of staff is an official refutation of that brain wave of some excited brother in arms or a clear afterthought, with a fatal mistake in it.

About the hour of noon Col. Dilworth, who had succeeded Col. McCook and Col. Harmon, in quick succession, in command of the brigade, sent me word to drop the 52d back to a designated line about one hundred feet to the right and rear of its line at the crest. This line is indicated in my work of 1903 herein and I am not interested in re-stating any portion of that work. With this chapter, it leaves the ground from the right of the big tree to the left of the tunnel opening in the line of our 52d breastworks and in front thereof to the rebel works unoccupied by any others than ourselves, from start to finish of Kenesaw and in possession of the 52d O.V.I. so far as it was taken and held by any Federal troops during any portion of the time in Kenesaw.

It is a fact that the 52d O.V.I. clung to the crest and slope of Kenesaw Mountain under the guns of Cheatham's men when every other fighting man of the Third Brigade was driven back and they were scattered down the slope and across the little meadow on the way to defeat and rout such as Harker's brigade sustained there that day.[30]

No human being has ever heard me reflect on the character, reputation or conduct of a man, or company, or regiment of the Third Brigade, of any rank, that day, and I wish it distinctly understood that I have no such reflection to cast, outside of what I may say of the little bunch of marplots and haters of Dan McCook and the 52d, some of whom are still alive and active.

The marplots mentioned have engineered the location of the monument to Illinois soldiers on Kenesaw Mountain dedicated on the 27th of June 1914. They have planted that monument, as already suggested, on ground which Illinois troops neither captured nor held during the assault

Movements and Positions in the Battle of Kennesaw Mountain

or siege of June 27th—July 2d, 1864, and which the 52d O.V.I. seized and held exclusively through that fateful period. The monument stands on ground between the tunnel mouth, which was opened at the bottom of our breastworks and in the left wing of Company B, 52d Ohio, and the ground covered by that company in its charge up to the rebel works. The shaft of the monument stands between the tunnel mouth and the site of the tree which tree had wholly disappeared in May 1897, but the margin of the foundation on the east is made to extend over a part of the site of that big tree.

There is no criticism of the memorial structure itself; nothing is volunteered or ventured in that respect; it is a matter of taste in which others are supreme and independent. The State of Illinois had a right to celebrate its Kenesaw heroes by any sort of erection it might choose, but, on behalf of Ohio and Ohio troops that fought and died there, Col. Dan McCook and the 52d O.V.I., I challenge the right and the act of Illinois, instigated and engineered by those who knew the wrong they were inspiring and perpetrating, to appropriate to the exclusive use of Illinois for the glory of Illinois soldiers a spot of ground over which they never fought or marched and over which Ohio soldiers exclusively charged and fought.

The work of the fine Italian hands of the Head Quarters Cooks of 1863 is perpetuated through the half century and its cuckoo character in the location of this Illinois monument is fully understood and appreciated.

Illinois, so engineered and misled by the malign spirit of the clique, may plant its Kenesaw monument on the ground which the 52d Ohio alone bravely held while Illinois soldiers were going at breakneck speed down the Kenesaw slope in a rushing, demoralized retreat before the enemy's guns; it cannot change and shall not pervert or obliterate or obscure the facts by setting its foot or its monument on ground which it never by a drop of blood or a wound consecrated and which Ohio exceptionally consecrated by its blood and bravery and skill, while Illinois in headlong flight had abandoned all as lost. The author, as did the participating officers and men of his regiment, saw, on that day, what he is stating in the way of facts like Aeneas in the siege of Troy, *quorum pars fuit*.[31] He had full command of the 52d Ohio from the moment it lay down nearest the rebel works, about 9:20 a.m. June 27th, 1864, until about 4 p.m. of

Chapter Two

that day, and he was never separated from the regiment, never had his clothes off, never changed a garment, never left the regimental line, never was off duty, did his very little sleeping in the trench which it dug, from 7 a.m. June 27th until 7 a.m. July 3d, 1864, and there were 519 52d Ohio soldiers, who could say the same things, except the one hundred and eight gallant comrades who fell in that assault and siege. Fate made some portions of their stories, on that field, more tragic, more pathetic, but none of them was less heroic or less glorious.

The Illinois monument stands on our ground without an atom of legal or moral right so to do. Its place should be on ground which its boys trod and stained with their blood that day, or those days, north and east of where they have set it some fifty or more feet in order appropriately to plant it on soil hallowed by the blood of Col. Harmon, Capt. Fellows,[32] and their fallen comrades of the 85th, 86th and 125th.

It was sinning in the face of light and knowledge for the schemers to make the State of Illinois believe that its monument should appropriate and occupy that spot and it is a gross mistake for those schemers to suppose that they can ever, by hook or crook, induce a 52d man who was there and still retains his mental faculties to ratify the rape of the monument location.

Let me take up the history of the tunnel briefly. It was located in the line of Company B, the left flanking company, of the 52d Ohio, near the middle of its line, but nearer its left. The suggestion and plan of a tunnel to the "Key Point" of the rebel breastworks originated with two Company B men and they were its engineers. The work was begun that day—June 29th—and pressed diligently every hour, day and night, until the rebels were found to have abandoned the Kenesaw Mountain line on the morning of July 3d.

I had taken Company G, 103 men, into the service. Two thirds of them had been students of mine in the Richmond college and knew them all personally and well. Captain Rothacker, a leading physician of the Richmond country, had succeeded to the Captaincy upon my promotion to major at the beginning of May 1863. Company B, next to him on the left, was from the Smithfield country, some eight or nine miles west of Richmond and my old home twenty miles away, and I was well acquainted with nearly all its men or their families when we entered the service. When we

Movements and Positions in the Battle of Kennesaw Mountain

settled down again to fortify the line it was natural that I should establish my headquarters, so far as I could have any, with Captain Rothacker and his boys. This brought me as a close and hourly observer of the progress of the work on the tunnel as it progressed, perhaps a half dozen 125th Illinois men, who had skill and experience in engineering and such underground work dropped in and at times helped with the excavation—the tunneling—and others of the 52d and 125th helped with the wasting of the material, brought out, down the 125th trench and over its headlogs to the west or southwest.

The work went on for a day or more undetected, but presently Johnny's sharp eyes noticed that the clay and gravel tossed over the 125th works, down the hill, were of a different color and quality from those thrown out of [the] 125th trench itself and they speedily reasoned out the tunnel plan that was being executed by the Yanks. The 52d and the 125th furnished all the men who worked on the tunnel.

When rebels abandoned their works, the tunnel miners reported to me that they were within from sixteen to twenty feet of the angle in the rebel works under which it was proposed to place the mine for explosion on the 4th of July. I remember the assurance of one of the Company B engineers when he reported progress on July 2d: "We'll have plenty of time to tunnel the rest of the way." No doubt the tunnel is there today almost as good as new after fifty-one years.

The resume, then, so far, of the matter, which has called out this second chapter of Kenesaw, is like this:

The first chapter was written in 1903 and the reasons for it are stated therein; there was then no provocation for the 52d Ohio man, or any other, to go into the subject or items disclosed and discussed in this paper, and if the Illinois monument on Kenesaw had not been constructed, or if it had been built on *Illinois* ground, as herein defined, this chapter never would have been written and the first would not have seen the light of day in the author's lifetime.

The "provocation" was the location of the Illinois memorial, not on Illinois, but on Ohio, ground on Kenesaw Mountain, in the sense and for the reasons stated in this chapter. No such thing was ever anticipated even as a possibility.

In that famous charge, Illinois troops set no foot and discharged no

Chapter Two

gun on the ground where that state has erected its monument. Ohio soldiers saved that specific ground and fortified and fought over it from June 27th to July 3d, 1864, uninterruptedly, day and night.

The design of the schemers in the location of the monument was the displacement and obliteration, as far as possible, of the credit and glory of the 52d Ohio and the appropriation of them in history, in future estimation, to the three Illinois regiments mentioned.

It was the design of the schemers to mix and boggle and befuddle the situation there, so that when those who had been in the charge and siege and knew what happened, passed away, the visitors to the battle field and the historians might credit the Illinois troops with doing a thing on that ground which they never did; might set aside and cause to be utterly forgotten the things they actually did and might cause it to be believed that they had done what the 52d alone had done. It was a most beggarly thing to do.

The charge began at 8:30 a.m. at a jog trot, double-quick step.

There was no halt, no obstruction, until the lying down in the little field in the bottom on the line of the tall stump mentioned.

The 52d after that—from that line—moved at the quick step—not a double-quick—without a halt, until it sank down in line under the rifles of the enemy, within fifty to seventy feet of the Confederate breastworks, not a regiment, company or platoon of Illinois troops in front of it; all were gone.

It lay in that line approximately a half hour and then craw-fished about thirty feet to the protection of an earlier undiscovered and then almost imperceptible crest, already described.

Lying at this crest until approximately the hour of noon, under the orders of Col. Dilworth, then commanding the brigade, the 52d moved about one hundred feet to its rear and right toward Mitchell's brigade, which, on our right, in the woods, going up against the fortified rebel line, had been repulsed, suffering heavy losses. It was lying in the woods where it later fortified and its works will even now show what its position was after the repulse.

Clancy, in one of the lulls of the firing, came over the crest and joined the 52d about 3:30 p.m. and at 4 p.m. the 52d was, by Col. Dilworth's order, moved back front and left to its line at the crest and that line was

Movements and Positions in the Battle of Kennesaw Mountain

extended to the left beyond the big tree and beyond what afterward became the tunnel mouth.

That line was fortified by the 52d Ohio and held by it continuously until the morning of July 3d, 1864; it never moved or changed its position from that time until it moved out of its breastworks July 3d, next ensuing.

An Illinois officer, who commanded one of the regiments of the Third Brigade made up a war diary, copy of which is in my possession.[33] In the light of the facts that composition is unique.

No mention is made in it of any repulse or break to the rear from the rebel breastworks of his Illinois regiment—not a syllable.

As I state, the alleged diary was "made up" and it is self-evident that the bulk of it was written by the officer long—many years—after the war ended; he himself shows that fact in his introductory statement.

Now, let us look at some of the text; a very little, comparatively, will be sufficient.

He says we moved out of that camp at 7 a.m. and charged at 8:30 a.m. of Monday, June 27th, 1864. It was only a few rods from that Sunday camp to the ridge on which we lay down near Gen. Thomas's head quarters and from which we started on the charge. I do not know what was done with that hour and a half lying within reach of rebel sharp-shooters. I do know that the time consumed is overstated, largely; but pass that; it was easy to mistake as to the time.

He says, we passed "down a Steep hill through Brush and Briars." It was a cleared, cultivated field until we came to the fringe of trees and bushes along the south bank of the creek. It was hardly a "Steep" field, but let that pass also.

Now I must quote his text literally for a space:

> Over Our Breast works [Gen. Morgan's] then Over a Slough, up through an Open Field, the 85 Illis. Comdg. by Col Dillsworth had his Regt Deployed as Skirmishers he having driven in the Rebble Skirmish Line, he fell in with Our Column then up a Hill to the Rebble works being on the top of the Ridge, here we Encountered the Rebble works, a Volley of Bulletts the Men presed on to the Side of the works, the Rebbles threw Stones axes Spades Clubs &c. the Brigades on Our Right and Left had falen back. Col. Dan McCook was wounded, Col Harmon killed, Capt Fellows of McCooks Staff killed, and about 400 Men Killed and wounded in Our Brigade. So we could not take the Rebble works we Moved back 35 yds under the

Chapter Two

Crest of the Hill and fought them while Some of Our Men Shoved up Chuncks of wood and Rails for protection. Col Dillsworth Learning that McCook was wounded & Harmon Killed he assumed Command, Sending General Davis word of Our Condition he sent us Entrenching Tools when we Shoon had three Lines of Breast Works thrown up Ready to Defend Our Selves and hold the Ground we had taken, the 86 Lost in killed wounded and Missing 98 Men in this Desperate Charge.... the 125 Remained on the front Line, we Carried off Nearly all Our wounded and Many of the killed."

Then follow more than five large type-written pages of names and ranks of men and officers killed and wounded in this regiment, in the body of which, after the list of killed, is thrown this bit of text: "I dedicate these two pages to Our dead Comrades, they Fought their last Battle, God bless them they wer Brave Soldiers and Neibours of Mine, and died Fighting for their Flag and Country."

A review of this history, so called, of that 27th of June, in detail, would be interesting if life were not so short.

The Morgan breastworks which he mentions were down in the field, and a little to our right, 225 yards from the ridge where we started on the charge. If any portion of the 52d saw them it was the extreme of the right wing of the regiment. The 52d, as a regiment, neither saw nor climbed those works in the course of the charge.

The alleged slough was the bed of a little stream called Noyes Creek[34] and it was a misnomer to call it a slough; our shoe soles were not wet, except where a boy did not care to jump, or hop across the little stream of water.

He says "up through an Open Field." That field was and is practically as level as a barn floor, showing that the memory was at fault in the attempted recital made many years after the event.

Col. Dilworth's regiment came in from the skirmish line and led the column up the hill.

The rebel works were on top of the ridge, that was true, but the volley of bullets did not wait until the brigade was "on top of the Ridge." "The men presed on to the Side of the works." This was literally true. The Illinois regiments struck not the point, but the side of the angle on their right. The modern effort to shift the Illinois regiments to the left so as to make them strike the point of the angle, so to speak, comes too late and must make a dead failure while any of the 52d Ohio live and remember.

It was not giving an accurate impression of the facts to make believe

Movements and Positions in the Battle of Kennesaw Mountain

that the Illinois regiments had stood fast while Mitchell's and Harker's brigades had fallen back from them. Harker's brigade went clear back on the left because it was not possible for it to stay on the ground and live; enough of them died as it was, the General being shot from his horse close up to the rebel works. Mitchell, with as brave a body of men as ever drew breath, was driven back, not in disorder, to the same line to which and back of it, the Illinois regiments were, not to their discredit, driven to disorder. It is not true, as implied, that the Second Brigade, failed, in any wise, to support the Illilnois regiments of the Third Brigade. I knew well many of the men and officers of the Second Brigade, even from boyhood on down to the end of the war and the survivors, even to this day. They were driven back part way down the hill with some heavy and deplorable losses, but I repel the implications of this paragraph from the testimony of my own eyes. The sketch maps of chapter one show facts, and they were made before I had any hint of the work of this Illinois officer.

I must requote: "so we could not take the Rebble works we Moved back 35 yds under the Crest of the Hill and fought them while Some of Our Men shoved up Chuncks of wood and Rails for protection."

This is marvelous for the commander of one of those Illinois regiments who was a participant in that assault. That they could not carry the rebel works was like God's truth. Human effort, at its supreme limit, could not do more. The heroism they had displayed was of the highest type; the ages to come would demand no more of them, and, in history, would mark the assault with Marathon and Thermopylae, with the sunken road and the charge of the Old Guard at Waterloo, with Plevna and Port Arthur.

It was not the truth that they moved back down the hill 35 yards only or that from thence they fought the enemy while some of the men shoved up chunks of wood and rails for protection. The story is told in the foregoing text and maps. In my mind's eye I can now see this officer and his regimental line after they pulled up their retreat and pulled themselves together into line well down toward the rebel rifle pits, in the edge of the woods, further to the rear than the front regiments of Mitchell's brigade in a position where they could not have fought the enemy without shooting the 85th Illinois or the 52d Ohio.

Col. Dilworth and his chief of staff about 4 p.m. finally fixed and

Chapter Two

established the lines of the 52d Ohio and on its right the 85th Illinois, slightly refused, following the slight curve around the crest, and then it was, not till then, that the 52d and 85th boys began to push sticks and stones and little limbs of trees "and chunks" up above their heads and to dig the earth loose with their bayonets and reach carefully back and down to their haversacks for their plates and tin cups with which to scoop up and toss above their heads toward the enemy the loosened earth—all the time the deadly rifles of rebel marksmen were killing and wounding wherever there was an exposure of any portion of a "Yankee's" person.

That line stated at "35 yds" was never the line of that officer's regiment unless he measured from the extreme right of the 85th Illinois after its line was established at the crest on the right of the 52d, and the 85th held that line, as suggested, in this chapter. Sergt Henry J. Aten of Hiawatha, Kansas, will remember whether or not the 85th gave place, in the front line, at any time, to any other regiment.[35] For the 52d, I cannot allow that the men of any other regiment "pushed chunks" or "tin panned or tin cupped earth" over a line between it and the firing rebels from June 27th to July 3d, 1864.

Gen. Davis sent entrenching tools, but not a tool until nightfall; the bayonets and tin plates and cups and hands of the men did all the entrenching and fortifying that were done there down to that hour; and the three lines of breastworks were never constructed by our brigade; it was a miscount.

The report which Col. Dilworth is said to have sent to Gen. Davis was carried as we have seen, by the chief of staff, Captain Anderson, and delivered to Gen. Thomas, in person.

"The Ground we had taken" hardly gives much actual information as to what occurred. It is liable, as the lawyers say, to a motion to make definite and certain.

"The 125 [Illinois] remained on the front Line."

This statement depends for its truth on what line is meant. It was not on the front line from the time of the repulse until nightfall. It was assigned to the front line at nightfall of the 27th of June and held that line alone until 1st Lieut. David F. Miser of Company G, 52d O.V.I, fell just behind its left wing mortally wounded, July 2d, next ensuing.

Its position from the time of the repulse until it began the work of

Movements and Positions in the Battle of Kennesaw Mountain

entrenching on the left of the 52d Ohio, down the slope, is indicated in the sketch maps in chapter one herein.

Now we come back to the alleged diary of the Illinois regimental officer. He says:

> [1864] June 28. Tuesday Morning Clear and hot
> the 86 Releived the 125 Illis on the front Line before daylight, keeping up a Brisk fire all day, Loosing 2, Benjamin Prentice of Company C Killed Sergeant Major Darwin E Ward wounded, we threw Out 15 feet in front of Our front two Pickett posts, fighting all knight[.]

This is a literal copy of the entry for this day in the alleged diary; we do not know how long after the war it was made; perhaps we can approximate the time, presently.

We know where the 125th Illinois line was fixed and fortified by the 125th boys from dusk of the 27th of June until daylight of the 28th of June 1864. This officer makes the 86th Illinois relieve the 125th before daylight the latter morning. The 125th had not been on that line according to this statement more than seven hours when it was taken off it. No reason is given for such change; none existed; the change suggested never occurred. If the 125th had taken the place of the 86th, which had spent the night covering itself with earth in the same way as the 125th and the 52d had spent it, the 86th Illinois had no need of headlogs, it was behind the 85th and could not fire over it; but let us follow these alleged "reliefs" and changes, on their own theory.

The picket posts were, in fact, in front of the 52d and 85th, and of no other regiment or regiments of the brigade.

The memorandum for the next day is in this exact form:

> June 29 Wednesday Morning Clear and hot
> the 86 was Relieved by the 52 Ohio, the dead Bodies between the works became so Offencive that we Entered into an armistice to bury the dead, So Our Officers Entered in to terms to Carry the dead to the Center, Leaving the Guns Lay and who Ever Carried the Hill of Course got the arms. after the dead were buried fighting Commenced we threw up another Line of Breast works Out as far as Our Pickett Posts with Cracker boxes and Old Barrells filing them with Dirt, we also Commenced Tunnelling to Blow up the Rebble works.

Why did the 86th Illinois need relief by the 52d Ohio? The latter had been forty eight hours on a stretch of front line duty and might have been

Chapter Two

supposed to need a little relief if there had been any such thing floating around on Kenesaw at that time, which there wasn't.

No reason is assigned and what became of the 52d in the relief unless it went into the original 125th works, down the slope on the left, is not shown or suggested.

No reason existed and no such shift or exchange occurred, but [by] following the programme the 86th is in the works of the 52d and the 52d in the works of the 125th, and the 125th behind the 85th, in the works of the 86th.

It was hardly the thing to style the two little picket holes, sufficient to shelter two men each for night observation, "a Line of Breastworks." They disappeared utterly long ago.

"*We* also Commenced Tunneling to blow up the Rebble works."

There are no specifications—"we killed the bear."

I have told the story of the tunnel unless I find that this diarist shows somewhere that I was not in the Kenesaw affair.

There is more of this sort of "brick work."

> June 30 Thursday Morning Cloudy and hot
> heavy firing all knight the 125th Ills relieved the 52 Ohio.[36] at One time we Expected they would attack Our works we lost two Men in the Brigade, the Rebble Batteries Shelled our forces but doing very Little damage A heavy Thunder Shower in the Evening.

The 125th Illinois relieved the 52d Ohio. Let us try to keep up with the procession. This supposed shift or exchange would carry the 125th into the works built by itself and transfer the 52d to the works built by the 86th behind the 85th. The 52d never was in those works.

> July 1 Friday Morning Clear and hot
> The 86 Releived the 125 on the front Line.
> we had this day One killed and 5 Wounded
> the Rebbles threw Stones Over in to Our works hurting Some of Our Men we threw them back they also threw Over Corn Dodger,[37] but no One was Injured by them. that knight they threw Over Turpentine Balls on fire So they Could See what we were doing keeping up a Light all knight.

The 125th wasn't then on the front line to be relieved, but, according to this man's programme, was lying in the second line behind the 85th in the original works of the 86th.

Movements and Positions in the Battle of Kennesaw Mountain

This supposed exchange of regiments left the 125th in the 52d works and the 86th in the original works of the 125th.

I pass the fun with the corn dodgers only remarking that it was a good long throw to send a dodger from the 125th line over the rebel breastworks and *vice versa* and to observe that the turpentine balls did not belong to that July 1st but to a night somewhat earlier in the year. The diarist somehow mixed or confused his dates. The turpentine balls notoriously belonged to the night of June 27th.

> July 2 Saturday Morning Clear and warm
> the 86 was Releived by the 52 Ohio we had two Men wounded to day Our Men kept up heavy firing all day and untill 2 Oclock that Morning, when the Rebbles Ceased firing, Col. Dillsworth Sent for me to come to his quarters he thought the Rebbles had Retreated presently a Rebble Called Over to us Saying he wished to Come Over, the Col. then Sent Over One Company to their works I went along and sure they had left, So Our whole army was apprised of it and was up Geting Breakfast.

He seemed bound and determined to make some change of location of some regiments every day, on paper, no matter if they did, in fact, stick to their own works, morning, noon and night. It was apparently important, in the diarist's view, whenever he may have done the writing, to mix the regiments up and confuse them as much as possible so that the special credit or glory which might actually belong to any one—the 52d, for example—in the charge, should be or seem to be shared by all.

"You may shut your doors against a thief, but not against a liar."

This was the last siege day on the mountain; next morning the rebels were gone from their works.

The diarist was careful, it will be observed, to restore the 52d and the 86th to their own works, respectively.

Isn't it a little strange that neither the 85th Illinois, nor the 22d Indiana was budged nor once relieved from June 27th to July 2d? They were liable to stock standing still in the one place so long on the theory of this chronicler, and yet he gives them no attention, does not even name either of them.

No regiment spelled or relieved the 22d or the 85th. They were not moved, did not even swap places, from their own fortifications, built by their own hands, at any time, in that period of six days' fighting.

The alleged movements of the 52d Ohio from the line of works which

Chapter Two

it constructed on Kenesaw in the night of June 27th, 1864, to the works of other regiments and back, at last, to its own, are pure inventions, freaks of imagination or worse—not one of them ever occurred.

I am not called upon now to enter into any controversy or explanation about the positions or movements of any other regiment of the Third Brigade, but I'll venture these statements out of my own knowledge:

The 125th Illinois was in its own works, built by its own labor, on the left of the 52d Ohio in full view of the 52d every day from the evening of June 27th until the morning of July 3d, 1864.

The 22d Indiana lay just behind it in its own works, not quite parallel with those of the 125th, through the same period of time.

The 85th Illinois lay on the right of the 52d Ohio in its own line of breastworks, constructed by its own hands, through the same period of time and the 86th Illinois lay behind the 85th through the same time, with the possible shift suggested, of which I had no knowledge and which I do not believe occurred.

This is an exchange of relief of which the diarist makes no mention.

The tissue of errors pointed out in this small section of this alleged diary or journal is designed to pervert the truth of history, to invent military movements which never occurred and which never entered into the purposes or the orders or the executive acts of any officer in authority on that field.

Whether the perversions and inventions are the sole work of the officer or the contrivances of some other for him is a problem. From my knowledge of the man, I could easily believe the latter.

Let us come as near the promised date of this diary as possible, with the data in hand bearing on it. It may be useful.

Its author wrote a letter to Col. John J. McCook of New York City, dated December 15th, 1902, which makes the introduction to his copy of the alleged diary.

After the date and address, he says:

> I have the pleasure after making a Copy of My Diary at your request, to say it is finished, and will express it to you....
>
> *A few years ago I made a copy* of the book, *and Each day* added the *Conversation and Incidents that happened*, which makes it more interesting to Me.

The italics are the author's.

Movements and Positions in the Battle of Kennesaw Mountain

Col. John J. McCook, of his own motion, expressed this book to myself in September, 1906. Having a *literal* copy of its 174 pages made at once for future reference, with no time to read any portion of it then, except his days at Kenesaw and at Peach Tree Creek, I promptly returned the book to Col. McCook, at New York City.

It closes with a biographical sketch of its author, winding up thus:

I will be _____ Years Old Februry 9th 1903
wishing you a Merry Christmas and a happy New Year
I remain Your Friend and Comrade signed _____

In April, 1907, I had my copy of this book strongly and neatly bound for future use, care and preservation.

From July, 1864, to December, 1902, was a period of thirty eight and a half years. "A few years ago" would not carry that work, which he described, back very far from 1902. The effective definition of the word is "a small number."

So far in the past were those "*added Conversation and Incidents that happened*" as to lose all shadow of pretence to a diarian character.

Before this branch of the discussion is closed, it will be proper to call attention to the fact that in his regimental report of the Atlanta Campaign—W. R.—this diarist officer makes no mention whatever of these alleged "releifs," thus showing that they were plain afterthoughts and inventions.[38]

One writer, who knew better, thirty years after the close of the war, speaking of that June 27th, said "Thereafter our regiments took twelve-hour turns upon the front line, firing almost constantly."[39]

He leaves a doubt as to his meaning. If he means twelve hour reliefs, then with three regiments on the firing line and two in reserve, it would not work, and the best that could have been done with the scheme would have been, while his statement calls for then, to make seven shifts or changes of each regiment in the Third Brigade, carrying it all over the hillside, in those five days. No such thing occurred, and, as Dr. Johnson said about a woman's "will" and "won't," "there's an end on't."

To sum up the point:

There was never a moment, from start to finish, after the 52d Ohio went to the ground, above the crest, at the end of the charge, that its rifle fire was interfered with or interrupted by the intervention of any body,

Chapter Two

troop or person between its line and the Confederate works, except during the cessation of firing while the truce lasted on June 29th, 1864.

The men who steered the location of the Illinois monument on Kenesaw could successfully crib the spot on which the 52d Ohio memorial should stand, or on which a monument to the Third Brigade, Second division, Fourteenth Army corps, might by agreement or consent of all parties, to wit: Battery I, 2d Illinois Artillery, 85th, 86th, 125th Illinois Volunteer Infantry, 22d Indiana Volunteer Infantry and the 52d Ohio Volunteer Infantry, be erected, but the special spot of ground which Illinois has exclusively jumped and occupied for its monumental purposes—hogging the persimmons—could only by such consent and agreement be rightfully taken from the 52d Ohio and appropriated or exclusively occupied by another, be that other the State of Illinois, the State of Indiana, or any corporation or organization of any name or dignity or character or quality whatsoever.

No special pleading can avail in favor of Illinois to justify such an appropriation and exclusion from that ground of the 52d Ohio as has been perpetrated. The right remains.

The schemers go upon the field, select the spot, build a monument upon it and inscribe and mark it as a monument of three Illinois regiments as the whole push, in the Kenesaw battle. A little more modesty on the part of the schemers, under all the circumstances, would have been a little more becoming.

If Col. Ethan Allen were living and describing the author of the grabbing of that foundation site for Illinois, he would say, as he did of a famous character, who offered the Saviour all the Kingdoms of the world, "when the d——d scoundrel didn't own a foot of it."

It was taking not only the highest and best seat in the synagogue, but it was an effort to appropriate, as the exclusive property of Illinois, the synagogue itself.

Exclude the whole of the Head Quarters Cook story and all its actors, the conclusion which is drawn simply from the things done on Kenesaw June 27th—July 3, 1864, and June 27th, 1914, as the climax of Illinois monumental work, stands unaffected. Illinois was made or led to bulge in and exclude Ohio from ground which Illinois never won or held and which Ohio both won and held.

The spirit and the men who engineered the location of the Illinois

Movements and Positions in the Battle of Kennesaw Mountain

monument have been truly depicted herein, no matter if they had never heard of "H'd Q'rs Cook."

It is six hundred and seventy five feet from the top of the ridge, where the brigade lay down, in battle order, to await the signal guns to begin the charge, down through the field to Gen. Morgan's brigade trench, and it is one hundred and sixty six feet from Morgan's trench to Noyes Creek.[40] I take these distances from Capt. Work's copyright map of 1902.[41]

In connection with the Illinois monument there was erected and dedicated a marble marker at the site of the Morgan trench on which are engraved these words:

> This marks the starting-point of Col Dan McCook's 3d Brigade, 2d Division, 14th A.C, in the assault on the Confederate works, to the east, at eight o'clock a.m, June 27, 1864.

The statement, so made on this marker, is untrue, whatever its source or inspiration.

Morgan's trench was the starting-point for nothing that morning.

The signal guns for the charge on Kenesaw were fired while the brigade lay at the top of the ridge six hundred and seventy five feet away from, and to the left rear of, Morgan's brigade, which was already in its trench.

On this new starting theory, what were the signal guns fired for? and why did we double quick all the way from the top of the ridge?

As has been described in each of chapter of this work, there was no halt or break of the double quick from the top of the ridge to the point of lying down, more than half way across the little meadow. The bank of the creek and the bed of the stream broke the step slightly, but there was neither slack or change of speed in the crossing of the stream.

We had traversed more than half the distance—572 feet—across the meadow before the halt and lie down 1150 feet from our starting point.

To style Morgan's trench as "the starting-point of the Third Brigade" is not only a direct perversion of the facts; it is a pure invention of some disordered mind, whatever the disorder; for what reason or under what inspiration, or influence, others are at liberty to figure out for themselves.

One might as well erect a memorial of marble or granite in the creek,

Chapter Two

or where the halt in the meadow occurred, or at the rebel rifle pits, in the edge of the woods, and engrave it with the words, "The Kenesaw Charge Began Here." There would be just as much truth in it and we all know there would not be an atom of it true.

Gen. Morgan lived in Quincy, Illinois, dead years ago; were the invention and the graving tool invoked fifty years after the war to give somebody some sort of boost with reference to Kenesaw which did not materialize that day?

It is rather late to start such a boost and is just as far out of time and out of line with the truth as to try to displace or distort the facts that we started from the top of the ridge, at a section signal guns down to our left and we never halted, for an instant, until more than half way across the little field looking up into the woods which shaded the Confederate works.

The 52d was a part of the brigade, the rear line, in view of all the others in front of it, in the charging column, from the top of the ridge to the top of the other where the charging column gave it—the 52d Ohio—the honor of the front line, immediately under the enemy's guns, and for a time gave it no support whatever.

That marble memorial marks the line of Morgan's brigade, which brigade was not in the assault, but the marker bears upon its body a falsehood in the effort to teach future generations that the Kenesaw charge started from Morgan's trench.

It did not do so by 675 feet.

The following are extracts from the report of Lt. Col. J. W. Langley, 125th Illinois, who succeeded to the command of the brigade September 1st, when Col. Dilworth was wounded at Jonesboro, twenty miles below Atlanta. 72 W.R. 710–711.[42]

> ....Eighty-fifth Illinois, commanded by Colonel Dilworth, deployed as skirmishers, with lines of battle composed of—first, the One hundred and twenty-fifth Illinois; second, the Eighty-sixth Illinois; third, Twenty-second Indiana; fourth, Fifty-second Ohio. These dispositions were made in an open field little more than one-half mile from the works to be stormed.... Col. C. J. Dilworth then assumed command.... After adjusting his lines to his satisfaction, he ordered works to be constructed, which was hastily done, and the front line of which did not exceed sixty yards from the enemy's strong line of works. The loss to the brigade in this bloody contest was 410 killed and wounded, nearly all of which occurred within

Movements and Positions in the Battle of Kennesaw Mountain

the short space of twenty minutes. These casualties fell heaviest upon the One hundred and twenty-fifth Illinois and Fifty-second Ohio. By 3 p.m. of this day the men were well sheltered behind their new lines of works and were confronting the enemy as sharpshooters. At 4 o'clock of the same day, upon my request to be relieved from duty at corps headquarters, I returned to my regiment and took command of it. From this point forward in my report I am chiefly reliant for information on the notes and memoranda of Colonel Dilworth, commanding brigade. After the confusion of the battle was over, the brigade was disposed thus: The Eighty-fifth Illinois on the right, connecting with the Second Brigade; the Twenty-second Indiana on the left, connecting with General Harker's brigade; the One hundred and twenty-fifth Illinois in the center, and the Eighty-sixth Illinois and Fifty-second Ohio in reserve, the lines remaining the same until the morning of the 28th, when the One hundred and twenty-fifth was relieved by the Eighty-sixth Illinois; that in turn was relieved on the morning of the 29th by the Fifty-second Ohio. On this day a cessation of hostilities was effected and arrangements made under flag of truce by which the dead between the lines were removed or buried. On the 30th a new line of works was constructed within from five to seven rods of the enemy's line. From this position our sharpshooters did excellent service, many of them using an invention called the refracting sight. The testimony in favor of the use of this sight at short range was abundant. The brigade did duty here until morning of the 3d of July, the enemy having again abandoned their works.

The order of the regiments in column for the charge is correct.

That Col. Dilworth assumed command is an accurate statement of fact; it was violently thrust upon him; his seniors in rank had been swept out of action and, with a few days of suffering given one of them, out of life.

That the front line did not exceed sixty yards from the enemy's works was true, but it was not a close guess on distances between those lines to make on the 9th of September, sixty-nine days after we had marched out of our Kenesaw works and through the enemy's works.

Sixty yards were one hundred and eighty feet; the distance between the rebel line and the 52d line as fortified was, as already stated, less than one hundred feet.

"By 3 p.m. of this day the men were well sheltered behind their new line of works." The Colonel did not join the 125th Illinois until after 4 p.m. I saw him come back to his regiment that day after several months on staff duty; he was not in the assault. He must have been misinformed about the condition of the Third Brigade works at 3 p.m. Not only so, the men were not so sheltered until after nightfall of the 27th when entrenching tools arrived on our line.

Chapter Two

I cannot believe that Col. Dilworth made such memoranda as is imputed to him and besides Col. Langley had no call to saddle errors on Col. Dilworth for he himself was in command of the 125th Illinois, and must have known, at least, what affected it and its movements.

After the confusion of the battle was over, the 85th Illinois was on the right connecting with the Second Brigade, but the 22d Indiana, while on the left, did not connect with Harker's Brigade, for reasons which have been shown and which everybody there will knew—Harker's Brigade was driven from the field and could not have lived connected with the 22d Indiana because of the topography, the conformation of the ground, at that point.[43]

When the confusion of battle ended and the assignments were made before, and fully executed at, dusk on the 27th, there were three regiments on the front line, as already described, the 85th Illinois on our right, the 52d Ohio in the center and the 125th Illinois slightly retired on its left. The 125th Illinois was never in the center and the 52d Ohio was never in reserve.

It would seem that the diarist above mentioned had borrowed the peculiar reliefs of the 125th Illinois by the 86th Illinois on the 28th of June and the 86th Illinois by the 52d Ohio, next morning; from this report of September 9th, 1864. They have been already discussed.

On the 29th the report locates the truce for the burial or removal of the dead between the lines, then comes a marvelous statement: "On the 30th a new line of works was constructed within from five to seven rods of the enemy's line."

"From five to seven rods," i.e., from eighty-two to one hundred and fifteen feet. The lines of the 85th Illinois, the 52d Ohio and the 125th Illinois had been constructed in the manner already fully described and completed in the night of June 27th, at the distances stated from the rebel works and those lines have been there ever since, except where dug or leveled down in these last few years. No such line of the 30th as the report suggests was ever located or constructed or can be found. There was no room for it; there was no call or necessity for it, and, to repeat for emphasis, no such line was constructed.

The diarist somehow overlooked the construction of this line of the 30th, but he worked in a relief of the 52d Ohio by the 125th Illinois in lieu of it.

Movements and Positions in the Battle of Kennesaw Mountain

Then the report takes no note of the relief which the 125th Illinois carried to the 86th Illinois on the morning of July 1st. One would think that Col. Langley, being concerned to mention the relief of the 125th Illinois by the 86th Illinois would not lose his interest in the subsequent reliefs, if they occurred, and especially in the 125th Illinois of which he was in command, in such close quarters.

The implication from both the language and the silence of the report is that there were no reliefs among the regiments after that of June 28th, which put the 86th in the works constructed by the 125th and, plainly, that never occurred.

These observations will suffice to convey definite ideas on the points set forth. As stated, this is not a history of the battle of Kenesaw, but is to protect the 52d Ohio against aspersions, distortions and misrepresentations, sought to be thrust into history to the prejudice of the Ohio regiment and for the false glory of Illinois troops. It has not been the aim or the purpose to take from any other regiment anything to which it was or is entitled. It has been the object to leave the credit and achievements of others unaffected and without any prejudicial reflection upon any of them, but it has, on the other hand, been the design to repel the groundless mistreatment of the 52d Ohio and the shameful slander of Dan McCook.

These two chapters carry the explanation, the reasons, severally, for their existence.

The first one was founded on the contingency of a necessity for its publication arising after the close of my life. It is the testimony of a participant, an eye witness to some things that the 52d Ohio had generously said little or nothing about and the Illinois regiments of the brigade studiously and forever ignored, as though no such things had happened on that field. It would be natural—human nature—that the Illinois regiments should not see some of them and quite as natural that they should make no mention of them, as they stood to the sole credit of the 52d Ohio.

But Omniscience only could have anticipated that the Illinois regiments would squat, with their exclusive foundation and monument, on that specific spot of ground.

When they did that, they challenged and invited this second chapter in self defense. They might so seek to monopolize for Illinois what never belonged to it and to appropriate or blur the credit and glory of the 52d

Chapter Two

Ohio there, but they shall not pervert or obliterate the history of what belongs exclusively to the Ohio regiment while they were making tracks—not cowardly tracks—to the rear and leaving the 52d Ohio there, under the enemy's guns, alone in its glory.

Harking back to the close of chapter one and Wellington's saying as to Waterloo and the playing fields of Eton, it may be said, with equal truth, Kenesaw was saved on the 52d drill fields of Brentwood and Lee and Gordon's Mills.[44]

Appendix I

At the annual reunion of the Fifty-Second Association, held at New Alexandria, Ohio, on the 20th of August 1897, I delivered an address, which, as it embodies the next day's "field notes," is given in full, as follows:

My Comrades:
In Conan Doyle's latest book, Uncle Bernac, he deals with Napoleon's proposed invasion of England in 1805. His hero, a young French refugee, crosses the channel to Boulogne and unites his fortunes with those of the Emperor, becoming a member of the court and, so, familiar with the great army of two hundred thousand officers and men there marshalled for the conquest, but destined never to set hostile feet on English soil.

Long years afterward, when that armed host had melted away in the furnace heats of Austerlitz, Jena, Eylau, Friedland, Eckmuhl, Essling, Wagram and Borodino and the remnant had nearly all perished amid the storms and snows and ice of the Russian Steppes; when new generations of the French had again furnished successors and waded through the blood and carnage of Lutzen, Bautzen, Dresden, Leipsic, Hanau, Ligny and Quatre Bras to the gloom and shroud of Waterloo; when the master spirit of those wonderful campaigns, broken and chafing against its prison bounds, the lone isle, through its last six years, had taken its eternal flight; when Monsieur Laval, stricken by the flight of time and with the infirmities of age, visits the camping grounds and the scenes of his early adventures by the French harbor, and returns from the review, he is made to say:

"Only last year I went back there under the strange impulse which leads the old to tread once more with dragging feet the same spots which have sounded to the crisp tread of their youth."

Appendix I

I plead guilty to this so-called "strange impulse." It is creeping down toward forty years since we began to make camps and marches and battlefields and history, in one of the world's greatest epochs; it is almost an average lifetime since all these things were finished and fixed as the eternal years of the God of battles, and it would seem to me no more a "strange impulse" to cherish and long to visit one's childhood home, or to yearn for the sight of the tomb of a child, or wife, or mother, or father, after long absence, or to see the faces and touch the hands of our truest associates and friends, when divergent paths and separate lots and lapsing years have neither broken, nor weakened the vibrant chords of enduring fellowship and confidence. It is *not* strange. For twenty years I have hoped to tread once more the same spots which echoed to the tread of our youth, to look upon the same hills and valleys, the same plains and mountains, the same fields and forests, the same creeks and rivers, the same roads and highways, the same cities and villages, the same sun and moon and stars, which, in that "elder day," we saw, in our most memorable years, through the veil of disease and danger, wounds and death.

I'll tell you why it is not strange. A recent writer comes close to my thought and I use his language, for the most part, dissenting, perhaps, from a very little of his doctrine, as it is expressed:

"It is with man as with nature. The chemistries of the soil and the sky are carried up into the plant, and are not lost but reproduced. The vegetable mold, with its forces and laws, is reproduced in the animal kingdom. So the animal life is reproduced in man, and enthroned with reason. The human spirit is a reservoir of storages and reproductions. The personal present is simply the full expression of the past. What we are to-day is a recapitulation of what we have gone over and known. Why should we have memory? Why should we linger over the past? Why do we like to think of childhood joys and sorrows? Why do we cherish the simple days when we put our little faces between our mother's knees and cried our discontent into refreshment? Why do we linger in delight over the barefooted tramps, the journeys to kinsfolk, and the school-day sports? Because the whole of all that was ever real of this is stored in us.

"These things are a part of ourselves. We can not escape them. They have had vitally to do in making us what we are. The flying years give us a sight of ourselves; and we see what they have done. An old man delights

Appendix

to entertain you with his childhood; and in so doing, he is simply bringing the record up to date. The fulfillment of more than he will ever tell you is there before you in his person and his spirit. So the past, not in its incidental and surface form, but in its essential value, is being constantly restored and reproduced. God finally weaves all the raveled ends into the fabric. The time of the restitution of all things is now.

"You start up a mountain road. The first day the flowers are in bloom at the base. The next day the sun brings out the same bloom on the next altitude, and the next the same; and after you have reached the summit, and look back, a great scene is before you. But more than this, that journey has become permanently a part of you. The road, the flowers, the rugged rocks, the cascades, the trees, the cloudburst, with every vision of your eye—all this has become a part of you never to be effaced. That picture, finer than human artist could furnish for a mint of gold, is yours forever. You return to the valley, you cross the seas, you live half a century, but that mountain scene, sunshine and all, has been ineffaceably placed on the canvas of your soul. That mountain did not absorb you; you absorbed the mountain. It will add richness to your spirit in eternity. In this way we take up and retain the essence of things, great and small, as we go onward. This is not because we will, but whether we will or no. It is not a question of preference. This law of human life would be fearful indeed were it not for the fact that the human personality is greater than all events. They shall not take the personality up into themselves. Time shall not, death shall not, eternity shall not; for the personality shall survive throughout eternity. Only it will be influenced in one way or another by all its events, either in time or in eternity."

I have two friends, who live in a western state; one of them far down the shady side of life, a minister of the gospel of peace, whose ears never heard the sound of warring guns; the other passed from the ranks to the head of his company during four full years of West Virginia, Maryland, Mississippi, Georgia, South Carolina and North Carolina campaigning. You know that was not featherbed soldiering.

The former, under no cloud, left this part of Ohio for the western home before the rebellion. The last message I heard from him conveyed the information, in general terms, that he had no desire to see any part of the State of Ohio, or any one whom he had ever known here. The other, who followed Horace Greeley's advice after the war,[1] wrote me last month:

Appendix I

"Haven't seen a battlefield since the war, excepting Siegel's retreat at Carthage, Mo., and do not want to see one. The war was the beginning of the end of this republic."

These two friends must be exceptions to the rule. They could not cry their discontents into refreshments with their faces buried in their mothers' laps, even if those mothers were living. The things which have touched their lives—many of them, at least—seem to have become no part of themselves. No beautiful or moving pictures, "sunshine and all," have been ineffaceably painted on the canvas of their souls. The mountains must have absorbed them, instead of their absorbing the mountains. While they should have taken up and retained the essence of things, great and small, the essence of the higher, grander life, possible to them, as been sapped by external and internal forces.

Neither would thank me for pity and I, therefore, waste none.

It is on the assumption that the rule and the exception are thus properly stated that I proceed. The very presence here of these comrades and their friends classifies them under the rule and not as exceptions.

At last, in a way, in no wise anticipated, came the partial realization of the long hope referred to. In May, with the best traveling companion any man can find on earth, viz: his "better half," I passed between two and three weeks visiting the principal camps and battlefields of the 52d Ohio Infantry Volunteers

J.T. Holmes, ca. 1915, approximately one year before his death (family archives).

Appendix I

from Camp Dennison, Ohio, to Jonesborough, Georgia. It is needless, in this presence, to mention even the principal cities along the line campaigning or travel. Their names are burned into each memory—Cincinnati, Lexington, Louisville, Nashville, Chattanooga, Atlanta. On this great thread, six hundred miles long, hangs the most of our military history. It was, proportionately, equalled in importance and intensity, however, by the succeeding, though briefer, chapter.

If spared in life long enough, I shall review that final chapter, in similar manner.

Upon a suggestion, for which I suspect that General Boynton of Washington[2] is remotely responsible, because I met him on Chickamauga field, at Crawfish Springs and at Chattanooga, my attention has been turned to my "field notes" of the visit to Kenesaw, for this occasion, though it must give anyone pause who undertakes to tell veterans of the civil war what they did on any given field.

In that famous struggle, this part of Ohio was largely represented by two regiments, whose numbers and deeds will be remembered and celebrated until the owl and the bittern typify the end of civilization and population over all these regions—the 52d and the 98th Ohio Infantry Volunteers.

At my request, my stenographer, with two or three small exceptions, has made a typewritten copy of them, with all their imperfections on their heads, and I bring them, as my bundle of sticks, to this annual camp fire, even though it is in the sultry month of August.

You will, please, remember that I write at our hotel at the close of day's observations.[3]

On the preceding afternoon, just before sunset, we had enjoyed, for some miles, the full view of both Kenesaws, as the train swept southward through Allatoona, Ackworth, Big Shanty, and around the eastern end of the greater mountain.

Appendix II

IN MEMORIAM.

We, comrades in the 52d Regiment, O. V. I., bowed under the mutual sorrow of a common bereavement in the passing of Colonel James T. Holmes from The Here to The Hereafter, desire herein to record a public and permanent testimonial to his distinguished military service and an expression of our devotion for his memory.

Ranking successively as Captain of Company G, as Major and Lieutenant Colonel of the 52d Regiment, O. V. I., and as Colonel commanding U. S. Volunteers, Colonel Holmes was tried in the crucible of war's tragic realities. As a leader he proved peerless in courage and in wisdom; as a comrade he was unfailing in sympathy, alert in assistance, a co-sufferer with his men in their every privation, always first in facing the foe, last in leaving the field.

Therefore, after half a century, we, the survivors of the 52d Regiment, in reunion assembled this, the 19th day of September, 1916, at Urichsville, Ohio, recalling the incidents of our memorable campaigns, attest with heartfelt pride that our Colonel, the late James Taylor Holmes, fulfilled our highest ideals of military honor and of exalted patriotism.

The private life of Colonel Holmes was one of peculiar loneliness, of great reticence, and of studious reserve. He asked little confidence and gave less. Born in Short Creek Township, Harrison County, Ohio, Nov. 25, 1837, enjoying educational advantages of collegiate and legal preparation, Colonel Holmes for more than two score of years was recognized as the Dean of the Bar of Ohio's state capital.

Appendix II

2.

In the midst of an exactingly busy life he yet found time for authorship, writing military memoirs, family annals, and biographical monographs in tribute to members of his own profession. He repeatedly declined public office, preferring scholarly pursuits in the seclusion of his extensive library to political fame.

It is in commemoration of a man eminent in peace and in war that we ask the adoption, by silent, standing vote, of the following resolutions:

1st.: Be it resolved that the memory of our lost leader, Colonel James T. Holmes, will ever be cherished as a most precious inheritance from our past and an inestimable inspiration for the future.

2nd.: That — "lest we forget" — a list of the campaigns in which Colonel Holmes took active part be herewith incorporated, in that the deeds of a man so truly great are his most fitting monument:

Kentucky Campaign,	August & September,	1862
Stone River, Tenn.,	December 31,	1862
Chickamauga, Ga.,	September 19-21,	1863
Mission Ridge, Ga.,	November 25,	1863
Knoxville, Tenn. Campaign	Nov. 28 to Dec. 16,	1863
Buzzard Roost, Ga.,	May 9 and 11,	1864
Resaca, Ga.,	May 14-16,	1864
Rome, Ga.,	May 17,	1864
Dallas, Ga.,	May 26 – June 4,	1864
Kenesaw Mountain, Ga.,	June 11 – July 2,	1864
Kenesaw Mountain, Ga.,	General Assault, June 27,	1864
Peach Tree Creek, Ga.,	July 19 – 21,	1864

Appendix II

3.

Atlanta, Ga., Siege of	July 22 – Sept 1,	1864
Sandtown Road, Ga.,	Aug. 7 – Aug. 12,	1864
Jonesboro, Ga.,	Sept. 1,	1864
North Alabama Campaign,	Sept. 30 – Nov. 15,	1864
March to the Sea,	Nov. 16 – Dec. 13,	1864
Savannah, Ga.,	Dec. 21, 1864 – January 19,	1865
Averysboro, N. C.,	March 16,	1865
Bentonville, N. C.,	March 19 – 21,	1865
Goldsboro, N. C.,	March 23 – April 9,	1865
Raleigh, N. C.,	April 13,	1865
Washington, D. C.,	May 24, 1865, Grand Review.	

3rd.: That these resolutions be spread upon the minutes of our Regimental Association, published in the local press with the proceedings of this Reunion, and a copy forwarded to the family of Colonel Holmes.

John Smith Pres
Lida K. Stewart, Sec

D. M. McCullough Chairman
W. P. Mulvane } Committee
Julius B. Work

140

Annotations

Chapter One

1. The New Alexandria Address refers to a speech that Holmes gave to the annual reunion of the Fifty-Second Association on August 20, 1897, in New Alexandria, Ohio, and which he included in this memoir as Appendix 1. He also reproduced this address on pages 171–75 of his combination travelogue and memoir, *52d O.V.I.: Then and Now* (Columbus, OH: Berlin Printing Company, 1898). The remaining pages he cited here, 176–201, cover Holmes's postwar recollections of the assault on Cheatham's Hill in that same 1898 memoir.

2. In a regimental line of battle, the senior major's position was on the left of the regiment, where he was responsible for the leftmost five companies. Holmes, as the senior major of his unit at Kennesaw Mountain, would have been posted on the left of the 52nd Ohio. See Silas Casey, *Infantry Tactics, for the Instruction, Exercise, and Manoeuvres of the Soldier, a Company, Line of Skirmishers, Battalion, Brigade, or Corps D'Armee*, 3 vols. (New York: D. Van Nostrand, 1863), 1:14.

3. Union Brigadier General Jefferson C. Davis commanded the Second Division, XIV Corps, Army of the Cumberland. This was the division that included McCook's brigade and the 52nd Ohio at Cheatham's Hill.

4. This was not Noyes Creek (or Nose's Creek as it sometimes appeared in Union reports), but a small branch of John Ward Creek. Noyes Creek was farther north on the battlefield, to the left of Oliver Howard's IV Corps. Near Howard's corps, Noyes Creek ran perpendicular to the Union position opposite the Kennesaw Line rather than parallel to it like the branch of John Ward Creek that McCook's and Mitchell's Men had to cross in their assault on Cheatham's Hill. The confusion of these two streams, however, was relatively common among the memoirists of events of June 27, 1864.

5. In this section, Holmes described the location of the military crest on Cheatham's Hill below and in front of the rebel works (discussed in the introduction). This section of Holmes's memoir also covers the movement of his regiment back to the safety that the military crest afforded after the failure of the union assault.

6. Captain Samuel Rothacker of Company G, 52nd Ohio.

7. These eight rebel guns were located just to the right of Colonel John Carter's Confederate brigade, south of the salient in the rebel line at Cheatham's Hill; they included four guns of an Alabama battery commanded by Lieutenant Nathaniel Venable and a four-gun Florida battery under Lieutenant Thomas J. Perry. See Hess, *Kennesaw Mountain*, 61, 119.

8. Colonel Caleb J. Dilworth assumed

Annotations—One

command of the Third Brigade after Dan McCook had been fatally wounded and Colonel Oscar Harmon had been killed.

9. Early in the initial assault on Cheatham's Hill, the commander of the 52nd Ohio, Lieutenant Colonel Charles W. Clancy, was wounded slightly by a ball that struck him just below his left knee. His doubled over boot flap prevented serious injury, however, and Clancy hobbled along behind the regiment, heavily bruised but still in command. As Holmes related below, though, Clancy did not fall back to the military crest with the 52nd Ohio following the failure of the initial assault because he was one of those men too close to the rebel lines to do so safely. He did later rejoin his unit, but he subsequently left the front lines to see to his leg. He did not return to his regiment until the next afternoon. As a result, Major Holmes commanded the regiment for much of the action on June 27. See also "W. J. Funston Recollection," in Work, *Re-Union*, 32.

10. As Holmes recorded in his 1898 memoir, Lieutenant David F. Miser of Company G, 52nd Ohio, refused to stoop behind the Federal entrenchments when he had to walk down the line on July 2. He was shot for his pride and died later from the injury. Holmes, *52d O.V.I.*, 186.

11. Holmes was quite correct in his conclusion that the mine commenced by the men of the Third Brigade played little role in the eventual Confederate withdrawal, despite his opposite assertion in his wartime journal (which he quoted previously in this early-twentieth-century memoir). The rebel retreat, as he suggested here, had more to do with Sherman's attempt to turn the left of the Confederate position. See Johnston, *Narrative*, 345; Johnston to Cooper, 20 October 1864, in *OR*, 38(iii):617.

12. Julius B. Work's only book related to Kennesaw Mountain was the compilation that he edited following the Third Brigade reunion in 1900: *Re-Union of Col. Dan McCook's Third Brigade, Second Division,* *Fourteenth A.C., Army of the Cumberland, August 27th and 29th 1900* (Chicago: n.p., 1901). However, nothing like the statements that Holmes summarized here relating to the 52nd Ohio's brief pause in the June 27th assault are found anywhere in this volume, and without further information, identifying the source of these remarks in unlikely.

13. Colonel Daniel McCook Jr., commanding the Third Brigade, was mortally wounded early in the assault on Cheatham's Hill, after which Colonel Oscar F. Harmon of the 125th Illinois took command of the brigade. Harmon was killed by a shot to the chest within minutes of assuming command, and Colonel Caleb Dilworth of the 85th Illinois took over. See Langley to Wiseman, 9 September 1864, in *OR*, 38(i):711.

14. Brigadier General Charles G. Harker died while leading the charge of his IV Corps brigade to the left of McCook's men. Harker was the only Union officer to lead his men against Cheatham's Hill from horseback, making him a hard target to miss for the Confederate defenders. Lieutenant Colonel James M. Shane commanded the 98th Ohio Regiment of Mitchell's brigade, which advanced on McCook's right on June 27, 1864. Shane was mortally wounded in the assault and died within an hour of his injury. See Hess, *Kennesaw Mountain*, 101; "Organization of the Union (field) forces, commanded by Maj. Gen. William T. Sherman, in the Atlanta Campaign, May 3 – September 8, 1864," in *OR*, 38(i):91; Pearce to Wilson, 9 September 1864, in *OR*, 38(i):693.

15. Some of the comments about Kennesaw Mountain in Holmes's letters may be contained in the twenty-five volumes of his correspondence available as part of the James T. Holmes Papers, MSS 765, Ohio History Center, Columbus, OH.

16. In a controversy over who was responsible for the American naval victory at Santiago during the Spanish-American War, Commodore Winfield Scott Schley allegedly remarked to Rear Admiral William T. Sampson that "there is glory enough for

Annotations—One

all," implying that no one needed to seek more than his fair share of credit.

17. See annotation number 12, above, on Julius Work's edited volume.

18. Holmes's specific reference here to "page 56 *supra*" is uncertain. He appears to be referring to the edited volume of Julius B. Work described above in annotation number 12, but that book contains no mention of Lieutenant Colonel Charles W. Clancy's return to the lines of his regiment, either on page 56 or anywhere else, though the event itself did occur. Like many of the officers and men in the Third Brigade, Clancy got caught in the no-man's-land between the Confederate line at Cheatham's Hill and the Union position that developed at the military crest. Clancy, like others, was initially too close to the rebel works to withdraw safely to the new Federal position. As the brigade's men at the crest began to maintain fire on the Confederate defenses, however, some of those men that had been trapped in no-man's-land slowly began to rejoin their units. Holmes asserts here that the 52nd Ohio's commanding officer made this return to the lines *of his own unit*, which Holmes saw as further proof that the 52nd Ohio was on the front line of the Union position during the afternoon of June 27, and *not* in reserve. See Stewart, *Dan. McCook's Regiment*, 119–120, 122.

19. The source of this remark is unclear. Holmes appears to be addressing someone else's claim that, after Lieutenant Colonel Clancy returned from the no-man's-land between the rebel and emerging Federal lines sometime on the afternoon of June 27, Brigadier General Davis of the Second Division, XIV Corps, sought a report on the actions and situation of the Third Brigade from *Clancy*, thus bypassing the actual brigade commander, Colonel Caleb Dilworth. All extant sources, however, confirm the same presentation that Holmes himself provided in chapter two of this memoir. After the failed assault and the accumulation of men behind the protection of the military crest of the hill, Colonel Dilworth sent the brigade's adjutant general, Captain Edward Anderson, to report the brigade's position to Davis and inform him that the unit could hold its ground. Anderson was also to request entrenching tools. Unable to find Davis, Anderson reported to army commander George Thomas, who could not believe that McCook's and Mitchell's brigades remained in such close proximity to the Confederate lines and so did not send the requested tools until he had confirmed the information. See James, "McCook's Brigade," 261; Aten, *Eighty-Fifth Illinois*, 186–87; Fahnestock Diary, June 27, 1864; Hess, *Kennesaw Mountain*, 151.

20. In his history of the 85th Illinois, Henry J. Aten implied that the brigade's regiments made no movements between their withdrawal to the military crest on June 27 and the night of June 29–30, a claim that Holmes disputed. See Aten, *Eighty-Fifth Illinois*, 189.

21. Aten of the 85th Illinois also claimed in his regimental history that his unit constructed an advanced line ten yards closer to the rebel works on the night of June 29–30, which Holmes also disputed. See Aten, *Eighty-Fifth Illinois*, 189–190.

22. Lieutenant Colonel James W. Langley took command of the 125th Illinois on the afternoon of June 27, after the regiment's colonel, Oscar F. Harmon, was killed while leading the Third Brigade. As Holmes noted below, until that afternoon Langley had served on the staff of the XIV Corps. In the final engagement of the Atlanta Campaign, Langley took command of the brigade when Colonel Caleb Dilworth was wounded; as a consequence, Langley wrote the brigade's official campaign report. See Langley to Wiseman, 9 September 1864, in *OR*, 38(i):711, 714.

23. Major General John M. Palmer commanded the XIV Corps of George Thomas's Army of the Cumberland until early August 1864.

24. Colonel Caleb Dilworth.

Annotations—One

25. Brigadier General Benjamin D. Fearing commanded the Third Brigade from the opening of the Carolinas campaign until the battle of Bentonville on March 19, 1865, where he was shot in the right hand. As a result, Fearing eventually had to turn the brigade over once again to Lieutenant Colonel Langley. See Fearing to Wiseman, 30 March 1865, in *OR*, 57(i):534–35.

26. Despite Holmes's claims to the contrary, his extensive discussion of the document makes it appropriate to quote at least that part of Langley's report on the Atlanta Campaign that covers the Third Brigade's actions at Kennesaw Mountain. Langley reported: "June 1, it [the Third Brigade] moved to the left and relieved a brigade of the Twenty-third Corps, remaining in this new position, under a constant fire from the enemy, until June 4, when it moved about three miles farther to the left and, with the division, rejoined the corps. The brigade performed the various duties imposed upon it (sometimes skirmishing with the enemy, building fortifications, changing positions, and holding works built by others), but all without taking an active part in any general engagement until the morning of the 27th of June, when it was disposed in order of battle as follows: Eighty-fifth Illinois, commanded by Colonel Dilworth, deployed as skirmishers, with lines of battle composed of—first, the One hundred and twenty-fifth Illinois; second, the Eighty-sixth Illinois; third, Twenty-second Indiana; fourth, Fifty-second Ohio. These dispositions were made in an open field little more than one-half mile from the works to be stormed. The Second Brigade was formed on the right, and General Harker's brigade, Fourth Corps, on the left. At a few minutes before 9 the command, "Forward!" was given, and responded to by the brave men of the brigade with the will and determination to succeed where success is possible. The movement began at quick time, and continued in this for nearly one-third the distance, when it was changed to double-quick. The lines moved with marked precision until they reached the foot of an abrupt hill, where they encountered a marshy creek lined on either side with shrubs and thickly matted vines. The command relieved itself as rapidly and orderly as possible from this confusion, and, turning its face to the enemy, rushed forward across an open field extending to within fifteen rods of the point of attack; here it entered a skirt of light timber, and from this point also commenced an ascent of the ground. On and up the brave men rushed, with their gallant leader at their head, until some of them reached the base of the enemy's parapet. Nothing daunted, they struggled to scale the works. In their efforts to do this some were knocked down with stones and clubs hurled at them by the enemy. Here the gallant Colonel McCook fell, mortally wounded, while present with and cheering his men on. Shot and stoned down, completely exhausted by the length and impetuosity of the charge, the brave men reformed their lines a few steps in the rear and partially under the crest of the hill. While this was being done Col. O. F. Harmon, of the One hundred and twenty-fifth Illinois, left the command of the regiment to Major Lee and placed himself at the head of the brigade; but hardly did he enjoy this command five minutes, when a musket-shot from the enemy pierced his heart, and in a few moments his remains were borne from the field. Col. C. J. Dilworth then assumed command, leaving the command of the Eighty-fifth Illinois to Major Rider. After adjusting his lines to his satisfaction, he ordered works to be constructed, which was hastily done, and the front line of which did not exceed sixty yards from the enemy's strong line of works. The loss to the brigade in this bloody contest was 410 killed and wounded, nearly all of which occurred within the short space of twenty minutes. These casualties fell heaviest upon the One hundred and twenty-fifth Illinois and Fifty-second Ohio. By 3 p.m. of this day the men were well sheltered behind

their new lines of works and were confronting the enemy as sharpshooters. At 4 o'clock of the same day, upon my request to be relieved from duty at corps headquarters, I returned to my regiment and took command of it. From this point forward in my report I am chiefly reliant for information on the notes and memoranda of Colonel Dilworth, commanding brigade. After the confusion of the battle was over, the brigade was disposed thus: The Eighty-fifth Illinois on the right, connecting with the Second Brigade; the Twenty-second Indiana on the left, connecting with General Harker's brigade; the One hundred and twenty-fifth Illinois in the center, and the Eighty-sixth Illinois and Fifty-second Ohio in reserve, the lines remaining the same until the morning of the 28th, when the One hundred and twenty-fifth was relieved by the Eighty-sixth Illinois; that in turn was relieved on the morning of the 29th by the Fifty-second Ohio. On this day a cessation of hostilities was effected and arrangements made under flag of truce by which the dead between the lines were removed or buried. On the 30th a new line of works was constructed within from five to seven rods of the enemy's line. From this position our sharpshooters did excellent service, many of them using an invention called the refracting sight. The testimony in favor of the use of this sight at short range was abundant. The brigade did duty here until morning of the 3d of July, the enemy having again abandoned their works. We marched through Marietta; thence in a southwest course about five miles toward Atlanta." For the complete report, see Langley to Wiseman, 9 September 1864, in *OR*, 38(i):708–717; the portion quoted above is found on pages 710–11.

27. Julius B. Work was a private in the 52nd Ohio's Company G. He was discharged due to disability in mid-December 1862, but after the war he was heavily involved in memorializing and recording the accomplishments of his regiment and its brigade. In 1902, he compiled a map of the Federal assault near Cheatham's Hill from a multitude of sources, and this map is what Holmes referenced here. The map itself can be found on page 27. See also J. B. Work, "Map of the 'Dead Angle,' Cheatham's Hill, Kenesaw Mountain, Ga., June 27 to July 2–3, 1864," in *Confederate Veteran* Papers, David M. Rubenstein Rare Book & Manuscript Library, Duke University, Durham, NC.

28. These letters may be in James T. Holmes Papers, MSS 765, Ohio History Center, Columbus, OH.

29. When he wrote that "I stepped from the line to the field," Holmes was referring to his promotion from captain, a company officer's rank, to major, a field grade. This promotion took place in May 1863 while the 52nd Ohio was camped at Brentwood just south of Nashville, though it was subsequently backdated to March. See Holmes, *52d O.V.I.*, 112–13.

30. The placement of Holmes's discussion of this new system of drill immediately after his description of his promotion to major while the regiment was at Brentwood appears to suggest that he implemented the new drill at Brentwood in the spring of 1863. In fact, it was a year later at Lee and Gordon's Mills when Holmes began teaching his men these new maneuvers. See also Holmes, "War Journal," 3, 9–10; Holmes, *52d O.V.I.*, 66, 157–160.

31. Lee and Gordon's Mills was on the southern edge of the Chickamauga battlefield where the Union right was located when that engagement began. It was also where the 52nd Ohio and the Third Brigade camped from March to May 1864, just before setting out on the Atlanta Campaign, and as indicated above, it was where Holmes taught his regiment a drill of his own devising. See Holmes, *52d O.V.I.*, 157, 168–69.

32. Holmes was overstating his own regiment's contribution to the Union assault at Cheatham's Hill. Its better alignment in the attack may have stemmed from its position

in the rear of the brigade. The rebel defenders may have concentrated on the brigade's more forward units, allowing the 52nd Ohio to proceed under a lesser severity of fire until it approached nearer the Confederate works. Additionally, it was clearly the topography and the poor location of the rebel line, not the Buckeye men's superior prowess at drill or their more orderly lines, that allowed McCook's soldiers to cling to their advanced position after the failure of the assault instead of retreating to their starting point.

Chapter Two

1. There is little evidence in the secondary literature of this alleged clique of Illinois officers unhappy with McCook's leadership, but that may simply be a function of the lack of a modern scholarly biography of McCook. Peter Cozzens, who has written extensive studies of the battles of Chickamauga and those around Chattanooga, has characterized McCook as overly ambitious and, perhaps, reckless as a brigade commander, but he did not delve into the politics of brigade leadership under the Ohio colonel. Moreover, there is no evidence, as alleged in the pamphlet that Holmes subsequently discussed, that McCook sought to inflate his own military reputation at the expense of the Illinois regiments in his command. See also Cozzens, *This Terrible Sound*, 121; Peter Cozzens, *The Shipwreck of Their Hopes: The Battles for Chattanooga* (Urbana: University of Illinois Press, 1994), 145.

2. Daniel McCook Jr. served briefly as the captain of a company in the 1st Kansas, fighting at the battle of Wilson's Creek in August 1861; he subsequently left that regiment and served on the staff of his brother, Brigadier General Alexander M. McCook, who commanded a division in the Army of the Ohio. The younger McCook, however, became ill after the battle of Shiloh in the spring of 1862 and left the army to recover.

When he returned, he began to recruit what became the 52nd Ohio. See Wayne Fanebust, *Brigadier General Robert L. McCook and Colonel Daniel McCook, Jr.: A Union Army Dual Biography* (Jefferson, NC: McFarland, 2017), 115–16, 118–19, 125.

3. Colonel David D. Irons commanded the 86th Illinois from the time it mustered into service in August 1862 until his death a year later. He was replaced as regimental commander by Allen L. Fahnestock. See *Report of the Adjutant General of the State of Illinois, 1861–1866* (Springfield: Baker, Bailache & Co., 1867), 2:306, 311.

4. The 69th Ohio was only temporarily attached to McCook's brigade for part of the fight at Chickamauga. The 110th Illinois was formally assigned to the brigade from October 1863 until early 1864. See Cozzens, *This Terrible Sound*, 543; Dyer, *Compendium*, 1093; "Organization of the forces under command of Maj. Gen. Ulysses S. Grant, engaged in the [Chattanooga-Ringgold] campaign," in *OR*, 31(ii):20.

5. As Holmes pointed out below, this seven-page pamphlet is "Head Quarters Cook," *Twenty-Two General Rules to be Observed by Colonels Commanding Brigades and More Especially by Those Who Aspire to the Position of Brigadier Generals, Compiled from Actual Observation at the Head Quarters of the 2nd Brigade, 2nd Division, Reserve Corps, Army of the Cumberland, Colonel Daniel McCok [sic], Commanding* (Chattanooga, TN: 1863). It is not necessary to reproduce it here because Holmes quoted the relevant portions accurately, and those segments he did not quote are of a similar character to those included. Also, the portions of this pamphlet that Holmes quoted below have had their punctuation altered from Holmes's to that found in an original, printed version of the pamphlet available in the Huntington Library, San Marino, California.

6. An Upas was a fantastical tree so poisonous that it was alleged to destroy all life, both plant and animal, for several miles around it. Figuratively, it refers to any de-

structive influence. See "upas, n.," OED online, June 2017, Oxford University Press, http://www.oed.com/view/Entry/219818?redirectedFrom=upas& (accessed 2 November 2017).

7. There seems to be little truth to this accusation that only the fixed bayonets of the three Illinois regiments kept the 52nd Ohio from abandoning the field at Perryville. Historian Kenneth W. Noe has written the definitive study of this battle, and his opinion is that the men of *all* of McCook's regiments stood up well to their first trial by fire at this engagement. The only possible factual basis for the anonymous pamphleteer's claim came around 7 a.m. on the morning of the battle, when McCook's division commander, Brigadier General Philip H. Sheridan, realized that Peters Hill, which McCook's men had just captured, was in danger of a Confederate counterassault. Sheridan stationed a veteran brigade behind McCook's and ordered its men to shoot McCook's soldiers if they withdrew without orders. These instructions, however, applied to *all* of McCook's regiments, not just the 52nd Ohio. See Noe, *Perryville*, 147–152, 278–283.

8. During the battle of Stones River in late December 1862 and early January 1863, McCook's brigade was part of the garrison of Nashville. During the battle Colonel McCook escorted an ammunition train of nearly one hundred wagons form Murfreesboro to Nashville with a mixed force that included the 6th Tennessee, two companies from the 10th Michigan, eight from the 60th Illinois, six of the 52nd Ohio's companies, and portions of the 3rd and 4th Ohio and the 2nd Tennessee Cavalry. On the road, Joseph Wheeler's Confederate cavalry attacked the train. About sixty rebel troopers reached the Federal wagons after driving back McCook's Union horsemen. As his own cavalry fled, McCook reported that "I endeavored alone to stem the tide—was completely surrounded by rebels—wounding at least one with my pistol." While the colonel tried to rally his cavalry, about two dozen Yankees drove back the offending rebels, gaining time for the 60th Illinois and 10th Michigan to deploy and drive off the Confederate cavalry completely. McCook's remark quoted here was probably the source of the pamphleteer's assertion here that the colonel claimed to have fought the Confederate cavalry single-handedly. See McCook to Wiseman, 5 January 1863, in *OR*, 20(i):445; Stewart, *Dan. McCook's Regiment*, 40; Reid, *Ohio in the War*, 2:315–16.

9. Blowing Springs, south of Pulaski, Tennessee, was one of the campsites of McCook's brigade as it moved south from Nashville in the late summer of 1863 on what became the Chickamauga campaign. The specific episode referenced by the pamphleteer here is unclear. Holmes described the marches both to and from Blowing Springs in his wartime diary and in a letter to his sister, but neither of these mentioned any kind of encounter with Confederate troops or southern guerillas. Likewise, Allen Fahnestock, then a captain in the 86th Illinois's Company J, mentioned nothing unusual about Blowing Springs, only that "our Scouts captured some old Shot Guns"; otherwise, he reported "Every thing quiett." See "Itinerary of the Second Brigade, commanded by Col. Daniel McCook, Fifty-second Ohio Infantry, for September, 1863," in *OR*, 30(i):872; J. T. Holmes to his sister, 18 September 1863, in Holmes, *52d O.V.I.*, 123; Holmes, "War Journal," 5; Fahnestock Diary, September 6, 1864.

10. The events described here involved attacks on McCook's command by Confederate bushwhackers as the brigade marched south from Nashville in the late summer of 1863 as part of the campaign that culminated in the battle of Chickamauga. On the morning of August 31, while the 52nd Ohio was getting ready to leave its camp just outside Lynnville, Tennessee, five Confederate partisans fired on and wounded two men from Company E who were filling canteens at a nearby spring. In retaliation, McCook

sent Colonel Oscar F. Harmon and the 125th Illinois back to Lynnville with orders to burn down five houses; by 8 a.m., it had been done and the brigade was on the road. Three hours later, near what Holmes called Pigeon Hill, three bushwhackers fired into the brigade's rearguard, which consisted of Company G, 52nd Ohio. The company immediately wheeled to the right and fired into the woods, possibly wounding two of the guerillas. Major Holmes then sent Company K into the woods in pursuit, and when he heard more firing, he led Company A after it in support. While pursuing the suspects, Holmes came to and searched a local home but did not find the offenders. While he warned the head of household of the dangers of supporting such partisan activities, his men set the man's barn afire without orders. Following these events, the 52nd resumed its march south towards Pulaski. See Holmes, "War Journal," 5; J. T. Holmes to his sister, 18 September 1863, in Holmes, *52d O.V.I.*, 121–23.

11. The anonymous pamphleteer was referring to events stemming from the death of Colonel Daniel McCook Jr.'s older brother, Brigadier General Robert L. McCook. The elder McCook commanded a brigade in the Army of the Ohio, and as it moved toward Decherd, Tennessee, in July 1862, it was set upon by Confederate guerillas. Suffering from a bout of dysentery at the time, General McCook was traveling by ambulance when the bushwhackers surrounded him. According to Federal reports, the partisans shot General McCook when he was unable to halt the frightened horses that were pulling his ambulance; the wound was mortal, and the general died the next day. Confederates, of course, reported these events differently, claiming that McCook was shot by regular southern cavalrymen while attempting escape. The northern public and Colonel Dan McCook, however, accepted the Union version of events. Regardless of the conflicting reports, all agreed that the man who killed the general was Frank Gurley. Gurley was eventually arrested, tried, and convicted of the murder, but he escaped punishment when, either by confusion or design, he was exchanged for Federal prisoners of war. In early September 1863, Colonel McCook's brigade found itself near the Huntsville, Alabama, plantation where Gurley was born and raised. The colonel dispatched Major Holmes and a mounted detail to destroy the plantation and all its outbuildings, except the slave quarters. See Daniel E. Sutherland, *A Savage Conflict: The Decisive Role of Guerillas in the Civil War*, Civil War America series, ed. Gary W. Gallagher (Chapel Hill: University of North Carolina Press, 2009), 83; Van Derveer to Flynt, 9 August 1862, in *OR*, 16(i):840–41; Fanebust, *A Union Army Dual Biography*, 73, 75, 77, 86–95; Holmes, "War Journal," 5; J. T. Holmes to Sue, 29 September 1863, in Holmes, *52d O.V.I.*, 123–24.

12. John J. McCook, another of Colonel Dan McCook's brothers. See Work, *Re-Union*, 82–83.

13. Unless the correspondence Holmes mentioned here can be located, it is impossible to ascertain which of the four captains whose last names start with the letter "C" and who served in one of the Illinois regiments of the brigade wrote this letter. The four possibilities include Albert Oscar Collins of the 85th Illinois, and Nathan M. Clark, Stephen D. Conover (or Connover), and George W. Cook of the 125th Illinois. It is possible that further research in the James T. Holmes Papers, MSS 765, Ohio History Center, Columbus, OH, may locate the relevant letters between Holmes and one of the McCook clan. See also Aten, *Eighty-Fifth Illinois*, 471; Rogers, *125th Illinois*, 183–84.

14. This 1897 trip was the basis of Holmes's combined memoir and travelogue, *52d O.V.I.: Then and Now*.

15. *Mens conscia recti* is Latin for "a mind conscious of integrity." Holmes was suggesting here that he was standing on his principles, regardless of what others thought.

16. Holmes might have been referring to the 1847 anti-war stance adopted by Thomas Corwin when, as a Whig Senator from Ohio, he refused to vote for appropriations to provide supplies for the American army fighting the Mexican-American War. While most Whigs opposed that conflict, Senator Corwin went further. When he gave a speech in the Senate on February 11, 1847, explaining his intention to vote against these supplies, he believed himself one of only three Whigs committed to that course, but when the actual vote was taken, only Corwin voted against the supplies. The Ohio senator, however, hardly remained isolated, later playing important roles in the 1848 and 1852 elections, serving as Millard Fillmore's Secretary of the Treasury, and returning to Congress in 1858 as a Republican representative from Ohio. Holmes, however, was likely suggesting that, like Corwin, he was acting on his principles, even if doing so separated him from his Third Brigade colleagues. See Josiah Morrow, ed., *The Life and Speeches of Thomas Corwin: Orator, Lawyer and Statesman* (Cincinnati, OH: W. H. Anderson, 1896), 48, 51, 53–55, 57, 59–64, 277, 285; Michael F. Holt, *The Rise and Fall of the American Whig Party: Jacksonian Politics and the Onset of the Civil War* (Oxford: Oxford University Press, 1999), 249, 261–68, 294–97, 526, 727–28.

17. This "Illinois officer" *may* be Lansing J. Dawdy of the 86th Illinois, who bought the land at Cheatham's Hill and who later served on the Illinois governor's commission that oversaw the erection of the Illinois monument. See pages 47 and 49 of the introduction.

18. John McGinnis, 86th Illinois.

19. This was the Kennesaw Memorial Association discussed in the introduction.

20. A *sou marquee* was a small, eighteenth-century French coin issued only for use in the colonies; in a general sense, it means something of little value. See "sou markee, n.," OED Online, June 2017, Oxford University Press, http://www.oed.com/view/Entry185120? redirectedFrom=sou+markee (accessed 25 November 2017).

21. Given the focus of this monument solely on the contributions of the *Illinois* soldiers at Cheatham's Hill, Holmes's ire seems at least partially justified. See also the photographs and discussion of that monument found in the introduction.

22. See chapter one annotation number 32.

23. The phrase "Movements and Positions at Kenesaw" refers to chapter one of this memoir, which Holmes wrote in 1903, a dozen years before he produced chapter two.

24. Holmes's quote was from James Montgomery's nineteenth-century poem about Arnold Winkelried, a legendary fourteenth-century Swiss hero.

25. From 1859 to 1862, Holmes served as president of Richmond College in the Ohio town of the same name. See "James Taylor Holmes," in Work, *Re-Union*, 87.

26. Lieutenant Colonel Charles W. Clancy remained in command of the 52nd Ohio until sometime after the failure of the June 27 assault. He first spent part of that morning and afternoon stranded in no-man's-land, and he subsequently left the field to see to a slight injury he had suffered early in the advance. Holmes, as the regiment's senior major, was stationed on its left. See also chapter one annotation numbers 2, 9, and 18, as well as Stewart, *Dan. McCook's Regiment*, 128.

27. The wartime letter that Holmes quoted here was also included in his 1898 memoir. See also Holmes, *52d O.V.I.*, 182–84.

28. In chapter one of this memoir, Holmes noted that this tunnel, which had been intended to extend beneath the Confederate works and destroy them with a gunpowder detonation, was commenced near the large tree he discussed here. The mine, however, was never completed.

29. See page 77 and chapter one annotation number 19.

Annotations—Two

30. Holmes again exaggerated here when he asserted that all the men from the Third Brigade's regiments other than the 52nd Ohio were "on the way to defeat and rout." Many of the men from those other units also clung to the ground near the military crest of the hill, seeking protection from rebel fire.

31. *Quorum pars fuit* is Latin for "in which I played a part." Holmes was suggesting that he was only making assertions about events at Cheatham's Hill in which he personally participated and, therefore, of which he had first-hand knowledge.

32. Captain William W. Fellows of the 125th Illinois was shot and killed just after Colonel McCook was mortally wounded and in nearly the same location on the battlefield. See Hess, *Kennesaw Mountain*, 124, 167.

33. This diary was produced by Colonel Allen L. Fahnestock of the 86th Illinois, and it can be found with his papers at the Abraham Lincoln Presidential Library in Springfield, Illinois. The weight of evidence, as discussed in the introduction to this volume, seems to contradict some of the claims Fahnestock made in his diary about Union regimental reliefs on Cheatham's Hill, but there is no evidence that he fabricated the diary after the war as Holmes claims. Holmes's accusations may have stemmed from the fact that, as he described below in this memoir, he was working from a *postwar copy* of Fahnestock's wartime diary that the former colonel seems to have supplemented with some postwar materials. The original at the Lincoln Library, however, bears no marks of postwar manufacture. Moreover, Fahnestock's practice of listing his regiment's casualties in the back of his journal but referencing them under the appropriate dated entry may have led Holmes to conclude that the diary was a postwar creation. Nevertheless, nowhere in the journal did Fahnestock betray the hostility towards Ohio troops or Colonel McCook that Holmes alleged. Holmes's subsequent quotations from this diary have been corrected to reflect the spelling and punctuation of the Lincoln Library original. See Allen L. Fahnestock Papers, 1863–1865 & 1902 (Manuscript SC 472), Abraham Lincoln Presidential Library, Springfield, IL.

34. This was not Noyes Creek, but a small branch of John Ward Creek. See also annotation number 4 from chapter one.

35. The history of the 85th Illinois by Henry J. Aten of that regiment mentions no movement off the front line between June 27 and July 3. However, as noted in the introduction, none of the sources that describe regimental reliefs in this period mention any relief of the 85th Illinois on the right of the Third Brigade's position, so this claim does not substantiate Holmes's argument regarding these rotations off the front line. See also Aten, *Eighty-Fifth Illinois*, 186–194.

36. The phrase "the 125th Ills relieved the 52 Ohio" does *not* appear in the originals of Fahnestock's diary. Holmes either misquoted it, accidently or intentionally, or he was working from a flawed copy. Because he subsequently discussed this misquoted assertion in his memoir, however, it has been left in the text as Holmes wrote it. If Holmes's copy of the diary *did* include this line, it could be evidence of a postwar attempt by Fahnestock to glorify the Illinois units at the expense of the 52nd Ohio as Holmes alleged. See Fahnestock Diary, 30 June 1864.

37. A corn dodger was a small cake of either fried or baked corn meal.

38. Holmes was correct that, in his official report for the Atlanta Campaign, Fahnestock made no mention of these regimental reliefs. See Fahnestock to Swift, 7 September 1864, in *OR*, 38(i):721.

39. Holmes was writing of Frank B. James, a first lieutenant in Company K of the 52nd Ohio at Kennesaw Mountain. In the 1890s James, who ended the war as a captain and brevet major, wrote a brief history of the assault on Cheatham's Hill and

the standoff that followed. In this work, which Holmes quoted here, James claimed that the regiments of the Third Brigade rotated off and on the front line in twelve-hour intervals, a claim that is not supported in the other available evidence on this issue. See F. B. James, "McCook's Brigade at the Assault Upon Kenesaw Mountain, Georgia, June 27, 1864, in W. H. Chamberlin, ed., *Sketches of War History* (Cincinnati, OH: Robert Clarke Company, 1896), 262.

40. As noted previously, this was a branch of John Ward Creek and not Noyes Creek. See also annotation number 4 from chapter one.

41. See chapter one annotation number 27.

42. See annotation number 26 from chapter one for all portions of Langley's report as related to operations on Cheatham's Hill at Kennesaw Mountain.

43. Holmes was correct that no unit on the Third Brigade's left could have connected with Brigadier General Charles G. Harker's men on its left because Harker's brigade had been driven back after the failure of its assault; it did not remain in position near the Confederate works like the XIV Corps brigades of McCook and Mitchell. See Hess, *Kennesaw Mountain*, 102–103.

44. See annotation numbers 30 and 32 from chapter one.

Appendix

1. Holmes was referring to Horace Greeley's probably apocryphal advice to "Go West, young man."

2. This was Henry V. N. Boynton who, as a lieutenant colonel, had commanded the 35th Ohio at Chickamauga. See Boynton to Beatty, 24 September 1863, in *OR*, 30(i):434–37.

3. Holmes was introducing the next section of his printed 1898 memoir, which contained his recollections of Kennesaw Mountain, but which were not part of this address. See Holmes, *52d O.V.I.*, 176–207.

Index

Numbers in ***bold italics*** indicate pages with illustrations

Adairsville, GA 18
Allatoona Hills, GA 19
Allen, Col. Ethan 125
Alum Creek, OH 6, 7
The American Family of Rev. Obadiah Holmes (1915) by Col. J.T. Holmes 1
Anderson, Capt. Edward L. 92, 110, 119
Andersonville, GA 37
Andrews, Lt. Col. John 72
Army of Georgia 16
Army of the Cumberland 13–15, 17, 20–22, 90
Army of the Mississippi 17, 20
Army of the Ohio 21
Army of the Potomac 14
Army of the Tennessee 14–15, 17–18, 20–21, 29–30, 43–44
Aten, Sgt. Henry J. 78–79, 119

Bates, Lucy K. (Kelley) 16
Bentonville, NC 16, 80
Big Shanty, GA 20
Bishop, Diana Graham 1
Bishop, Douglas Graham 1
Bishop, Elaine Mabury 1
Bishop, Garth Douglas 1
Bishop, Joyce Claire 1
Bishop, Quentin Holmes 1
Bragg, Gen. Braxton 12–14
Brentwood, TN 85, 87, 108, 131
Brown's Ferry, TN 14
Brushy Mountain, GA 20
Buell, Maj. Gen. Don Carlos 11
Burnside, Maj. Gen. Ambrose 14

Camp Chase, OH 11
Camp Creek, GA 18
Camp Dennison, OH 11
Camp Lew Wallace, OH 11
Carolinas Campaign 6, 79
Carter, John 25, 66–67, 104

Cassville, GA 18–19
Channel, Virgil B. 5–6, 45, 47
Chattahoochee River 19, 44
Chattanooga, TN 12–14, 17, 44, 80
Cheatham, Maj. Gen. Benjamin F. 6, **22**, 22–25, 36, 111
Cheatham Hill 5–6, 9, 23–25, **28**, 29–31, 33–36, 39–40, 43, 45, 47–50
Chickamauga, GA 5–6, 13, 87, 89–90
Chickamauga Creek, GA 13, 15
Clancy, Lt. Col. Charles 41, 42, 67, 77–78, 110, 115
Cleburne, Maj. Gen. Patrick 22
Corman, Amanda 50

Dalton, GA 18
Davis, Maj. Gen. Jefferson C. **12**, 14–15, 25–26, 33–34, 44, 62, 77–78, 94, 110, 117, 119
Dawdy, Sgt. Lansing J. 47, 49
Day, Clarence Shepard, Jr. 8
Dead Angle 24–26, **27**, **27**, **28**, **29**, 43, 68, 79, 93
Dibelka, James 49
Dilworth, Col. Caleb 30, **30**, 32–34, 43, 66, 77–79, 81, 89, 110–111, 115–119, 127–129
Dunne, Edward F. 50
Durham Station, NC 101

Etowah River, GA 19

Fahnestock, Col. Allen L. **32**, 35–36, 39–42
Fearing, Brig. Gen. Benjamin D. 16, 79–80
Fellows, Capt. William W. 113, 116
Forrest, Maj. Gen. Nathan Bedford 15
Frankenburg, Corp. Joseph 35, 41
Franklin College, OH 10
Funson, Pvt. William 41–42

Gilgal Church, GA 20
Granger, Maj. Gen. Gordon 13

Index

Grant, Maj. Gen. Ulysses S. 14
Green Lawn Cemetery, OH 16
Grimshaw, Corp. Sam 78
Gurley, Frank 13

Hardee, Lt. Gen. William J. 17, 19, 21
Harker, Col. Charles Garrison 23, 25–27, 65, 69, 81–82, 104, 118, 128–129
Harmon, Col. Oscar F. 29, 39, 49, 74, 79–80, 89, 106, 110–111, 113, 116–117
Harrison County, OH 9
Hess, Earl J. 32, 35, 38
Holmes, Abraham R. (A.R.) 10, 95
Holmes, Asa 9
Holmes, Constance Mabury 1
Holmes, Col. James Taylor (J.T.) 1–3, **5**, 6–9, **10**, 11–17, 20, 23, 26, 33, 35–36, 40–45, 50, **136**; see also Kennesaw Battlefield, sketches of (by Holmes)
Holmes, Lawrence Asa 4
Holmes, Mary McCoy 9
Holmes, Rev. Obediah 1
Hood, Lt. Gen. John Bell 15–16, 17, 20–21, 44, 106
Hooker, Maj. Gen. Joseph 14, 19, 21
Hutchison, Capt. Archibald B. 7

Illinois Monument **34**, **46**, **48**, 50, 99, **109**, 113–114, 125–126
Illinois Volunteer Infantries 11, 14, 26, 29–30, 32–33, 35, 37–43, 47, 49–50, 65
Indiana Volunteer Infantries 12, 15, 6, 31–32, 65
Iowa Wesleyan University 10
Irons, Col. David D. 89

James, Capt. Frank 38, 40
Jocko **5**, 6
John Ward Creek 21, 29
Johnston, Gen. Joseph E. 15–21, 39, 43–44, 106
Jonesboro, GA 3, 7
Jonesboro, Battle of 15, 44, 79

Kelly House (Chickamauga) 6
Kennesaw, GA 2–3, 5–6, 20, 44–45
Kennesaw Battlefield 2, 4, 6–8; purchase 95–99; sketches (by Holmes) **61**, **62**, **63**, **65**, **68**, **69**, **70**, **75**, **76**
Kennesaw Memorial Association 47, 49
Kennesaw Mountain 8, 9, 15, 17, 32, 37, 43, 45, 47–49, 111, 114
Kennesaw Mountain Battlefield Park 50
Kennesaw Tunnel 113–114
Kentucky River 11
Kimball, Brig. Gen. Nathan 25–26

Kingman, Martin 47
Knoxville, TN 16
Kolbs Farm 21
Korbel, J. Mario 49

Langley, Lt. Col. James W. 31, **31**, 32–33, 35, 37–42, 79–80, 82, 127, 129–130
Lay's Ferry, GA 18
Lee and Gordon's Mills, GA 15, 86–87, 109, 131
Lexington, KY 11
Little Kennesaw Mountain 20
Longstreet, Lt. Gen. James 13, 15
Lookout Mountain 14
Loring, Maj. Gen. William W. 20–21
Lost Mountain 20
Louisville, KY 11, 88
Lynville, TN 13

Madden, Corp. Michael 7
Maney, Brig. Gen. George 25, 26, 29, 33–34
March to the Sea 6
Marietta, GA 19, 106
McCafee's Church 13, 15
McCook, Brig. Gen. Alexander 89, 144
McCook, Col. Daniel, Jr. 10, **11**, 12, 15–16, 23, 26, **27**, 29–30, 32–33, 36–39, 43–45, 47, 49, 61, 74, 86, 88, 90, 93
McCook, Maj. Daniel, Sr. 10
McCook, Col. George W. 89
McCook, Hon. George W. 89
McCook, Col. John J. 89, 99, 123–124
McCook, Brig. Gen. Robert L. 13
McGinnis, Sgt. John 47
McPherson, Maj. Gen. James 17–19, 21–22, 25, 43,
Mercer, Pvt. Robert N. 7
Military Crest **23**, 24, 31, 32, 140–141, 147
Minty, Col. Robert 13
Miser, Lt. David F. 60, 72, 78–79, 82–83, 85, 106, 119
Missionary Ridge 14, 90
Mitchell, Brig. Gen. John G. 23, 25–27, 33–35, 37–39, 67–69, 75, 104, 115, 118
Morgan, Brig. Gen. John Hunt 116, 126–127
Mud Creek 20

Nashville, TN 12
National Bank Building (Columbus, OH) 3
Neighbor, Corp. Theodore 41
Nelson, Maj. Gen. Wilson 11
New Alexandria Address 61
New Smyrna, GA 44
Newton, Brig. Gen. John 25
North Chickamauga Creek 14
Noyes Creek 2, 64–65, 117, 126

Index

O'Donnell, Pvt. Edward 37
Ohio State Bar Association 4, 16
Ohio Volunteer Infantries 10–17, 26, 30–33, 35, 37–42, 44–45, 49–50, 61, 63–64
Olley Creek 22
Oostanaula River 18

Palmer, Maj. Gen. John A. 31, 39, 79
Payne, Sgt. Edwin 39
Payton, William A. 49
Pea Ridge, AR 105
Peach Tree Creek, GA 124
Peoria, IL 89
Perryville, Battle of 12, 101
Picketts Mill, GA 19–20
Pigeon Hill 20–21, 25
Pine Mountain 20
Polk, Lt. gen. Leonidas 17, 19–20
Pratt, Sgt. Henry 39
Prentice, Benjamin 120

Quincy, IL 127

Reason, Pvt. Horace F. 49
Reed's Bridge 13
Rees, W.T. 6
Resaca, GA 18
Richmond, OH 10
Richmond College 10, 102, 113
Ringgold, GA 13
Rocky Face Ridge 18
Rogers, Sgt. Robert M. 41
Rosecrans, Maj. Gen. William S. 12–13
Rossville Gap 13
Rothacker, Capt. Samual 7, 66, 82–83, 85, 104, 113–114

Salem, OH 72
Savannah, GA 45
Schofield, Maj. Gen. John M. 17–18, 21, 43

Second Brigade 38
Sherman, Maj. Gen. William Tecumseh 14–22, 39, 43–44
Short Creek, OH 9
Slocum, Maj. Gen. Henry 16, 44
Smith, Maj. Gen. Edmund Kirby 11
Smyrna, GA 44
Snake Creek Gap, GA 18
Stanley, Maj. Gen. David 25
Stewart, Sgt. Nixon B. 3, 42
Stones River, Battle of 12

Then and Now (Col. J.T. Holmes, 1915) 5, 7, 16, 45, 61
Third Brigade{e23, 30, 32, 33–35, 37, 39–40, 42, 45, 48, 59, 61, 64, 67, 72, 74, 82, 86–87, 89, 92–94, 110, 116, 133
Thomas, Maj. Gen. George H. 13–14, 16, *17*, 18, 22–23, 25, 34, 43–44, 110, 116, 119
Tod, David 10
Topographical Crest *see* Military Crest
Tullahoma, Campaign of 12

Van Tassell, Lt. Col. Oscar 38
Vaughan, Brig. Gen. Alfred 25–26, 29

Wagner, Brig. Gen. George 23, 25, 26, 28
Wagoner, John 10
Wagoner, Sarah 10
Ward, Maj. Darwin E. 120
Ward, Corp. Philip 38
Welt, Pvt. Joseph K. 102, 104
Western and Atlantic Railroad 18
Wheeler, Maj. Gen. Joseph 21, 91
Winkelried, Arnold von 102
Woods, Col. Joseph Jackson 6
Work, Capt. Julius 27, 42, 73, 77–78, 80, 126
Work Map *27*, 42, 80, 126, 143
Wycoff, Corp. Isaac Newton 102

www.ingramcontent.com/pod-product-compliance
Ingram Content Group UK Ltd.
Pitfield, Milton Keynes, MK11 3LW, UK
UKHW042016140426
5217IPUK00015B/1212